teach yourself®

For over 60 years, more than 50 million people have learnt over 750 subjects the **teach yourself** way, with impressive results.

be where you want to be
with **teach yourself**

For UK order enquiries: please contact Bookpoint Ltd, 130 Milton Park, Abingdon, Oxon, OX14 4SB. Telephone: +44 (0) 1235 827720. Fax: +44 (0) 1235 400454. Lines are open 09.00–17.00, Monday to Saturday, with a 24-hour message answering service. Details about our titles and how to order are available at www.teachyourself.co.uk

For USA order enquiries: please contact McGraw-Hill Customer Services, PO Box 545, Blacklick, OH 43004-0545, USA. Telephone: 1-800-722-4726. Fax: 1-614-755-5645.

For Canada order enquiries: please contact McGraw-Hill Ryerson Ltd, 300 Water St, Whitby, Ontario, L1N 9B6, Canada. Telephone: 905 430 5000. Fax: 905 430 5020.

Long renowned as the authoritative source for self-guided learning – with more than 50 million copies sold worldwide – the **teach yourself** series includes over 500 titles in the fields of languages, crafts, hobbies, business, computing and education.

British Library Cataloguing in Publication Data: a catalogue record for this title is available from the British Library.

Library of Congress Catalog Card Number: on file.

First published in UK 1997 by Hodder Education, 338 Euston Road, London, NW1 3BH.

First published in US 2001 by The McGraw-Hill Companies, Inc.

This edition published 2006.

The **teach yourself** name is a registered trade mark of Hodder Headline.

Typeset by Transet Limited, Coventry, England.
Printed in Great Britain for Hodder Education, a division of Hodder Headline, 338 Euston Road, London, NW1 3BH, by Cox & Wyman Ltd, Reading, Berkshire.

The publisher has used its best endeavours to ensure that the URLs for external websites referred to in this book are correct and active at the time of going to press. However, the publisher and the author have no responsibility for the websites and can make no guarantee that a site will remain live or that the content will remain relevant, decent or appropriate.

Hodder Headline's policy is to use papers that are natural, renewable and recyclable products and made from wood grown in sustainable forests. The logging and manufacturing processes are expected to conform to the environmental regulations of the country of origin.

Impression number   10 9 8 7 6 5 4 3 2 1
Year   2010 2009 2008 2007

contents

dedication

This book is dedicated to my parents, Maria and Alan, who lived the Way of Truth without ever needing to name it. My mother showed me the face of compassion and intuition. My father showed me the face of reason and clear thinking. I cannot forget my children Eve and Jacob whose *joie de vivre* is an example to follow. In their faces I see the future. Now I must thank Mike who showed me that happiness is the highest of goals. No student of meditation can forget the teachers who walked the path before and left their footprints in the sands of time. I acknowledge all their great kindness. I acknowledge the past but now I look to the future where I know a new tradition shall arise. I have seen the seeds of it and I am profoundly grateful to be alive at this extraordinary time.

sources

preface

Power to the People

> We speak at times of an expanding universe what we really mean is an expanding consciousness.
>
> The Tibetan, *A Treatise on White Magic*

It is an exciting time to be alive. We are living through a multi-dimensional revolution. Computer technology may be its most obvious sign, but this is indeed a revolution in human consciousness. Ideas and thoughts, questions and answers, comments and opinions now flash around the globe in a continuous stream of mental activity. In the new domain of cyberspace, information is free, knowledge is accessible, but wisdom is a rarity. Like winged Mercury, the ancient messenger of the gods, our thoughts have now taken flight and will never be earthbound again. Not only can we send a thought package at the touch of a button, but we can download images of the heavens and share astronomical experiences not available to previous generations. The perspective we hold of ourselves and our world is expanding continuously.

Rapid change can be unsettling. In a time of constant change, the opposing forces of resistance and propulsion are at work. The old and the new jostle against each other uncomfortably. Like the classic yin-yang symbol of dark and light, change and constancy are inseparably united and part of a greater whole. Embracing the future and releasing the past asks for openness of both heart and mind, which permits the unknown to take seed as the possible, and a transparency of being, which enables the past to be dissolved and makes space for growth and expansion. Openness and transparency are unusual qualities that are not taught through education, but gained through meditation – the oldest, most full, most rich and most valuable education of all.

The opportunities now available to the many are unique. Travel, whether physical through a real journey, or mental through a journey in the imagination, has a liberating and empowering effect on the rational and imaginative mind. In classical times the sphere of travel was placed under the aegis of Mercury, who acted as protector to pilgrims and guide in unseen places. His staff entwined with double serpents is still in use as a symbol for both healing and communication. Mercury as the winged messenger still serves as an appropriate guide to the shifting sands at our feet. Like the element mercury, which breaks and reforms in a continuous silver but deadly dance, messages have never been so constantly created and dispatched with such swiftness. There are dangers in information overload, we cannot handle a raw diet of continuous information, just as we cannot handle mercury itself without danger. The Roman Mercury was also the Greek Hermes, a very similar figure who also symbolized the role of a divine intermediary between heaven and earth. Whereas Mercury has a tricky and dangerous side, Hermes, in the same capacity as a winged messenger, has matured and left behind the playful and slippery characteristics of exuberant youthfulness. Mercury can be equated with knowledge but Hermes is equated with wisdom and takes on a greater responsibility as a guide to the inner world of the psyche, not merely to the vast realm of the mind. We are currently dazzled by the ever changing quicksilver realm of Mercury and the communications revolution. The swift and darting flight of thought and word, continuous mental activity, endless possibilities and technological wizardry are the marvels of our time. But thought without substance and information without meaning give no personal satisfaction, merely unending activity. We need the stabilizing guidance of Hermes, the ancient god of wisdom and patron to the Hermetic Wisdom, which has woven its way into Western history as a frail but vital silver thread. When we see the communication revolution as but one aspect of a greater revolution in consciousness, we can regain a footing. Change and constancy *can* coexist. Mental activity in all its many varied forms is attributed to Mercury, but the transformed and awakened meditative mind is attributed to Hermes. The path of knowledge can become the path to wisdom. The spiritual path remains as ever the guiding path through the maze of life's experiences. Meditative practice is the key to the generation of the spiritual path, which, even when it appears to be found externally, is created like a spider's silk spun from the depths of one's own being.

Meditation is flowering in the West upon an Eastern rootstock. The result is a new bloom, the hybrid creation of ancient technique and modern interpretation. This new *Rosa Mundi* takes its life from the stored potential locked away by the narrow life goals, materialistic philosophy and a dried out dogma that has gripped Western culture for too long. Like a spring coiled under ever increasing tension, eventual release brings a tremendous power and dynamism; release has come. The life-giving water of spiritual ideas, personal practice and holistic philosophy are as rain to the desert. This bounty has generated an unexpected harvest of ideas and practices most suited to our Western life. Yet flower and root cannot be separated, they are as one.

The Western meditation in which you are invited to share is a unique pot-pourri. Purists might indeed frown upon its eclectic nature, absence of lengthy training and informal organization, but this is indeed a new movement, it is Aquarian in every way. Organic and self defining it has none of the rigid structure of a defined and stratified hierarchy. What it lacks in age it compensates for in inventiveness, creativity and discovery. It is the genuine and spontaneous response to the deepest call of our times for personal meaning. This homegrown movement has produced its own gurus, John Gray, Caroline Myss, Jean Houston and Deepak Chopra, among many others, who teach not in the temple but through the workshop and best-selling books, cassettes and videos.

The wisdom that is being voiced is directly related to daily life, not temple life, and to the everyday issues of health, happiness, relationships and all that is encompassed by the world at large. The outstanding figures in the new generation of Western teachers bring gifts from the traditions in which they served as apprentices. Such teachers have distilled and redefined traditional practices for a new generation living out in the world bearing all the pressures of careers, relationships and family life. John Gray, author of the best selling *Venus and Mars* series, is in many ways typical of the new Western guru. As a celibate Hindu monk for nine years he spent more than 10 hours in daily meditation. Now this unlikely candidate has poured a new wisdom into the tired institution of marriage and has revitalized our understanding of what a loving relationship can be. His clarity, truthfulness and insight has healed thousands of relationships and enabled everyday folk to find meaning in life. He is typical of the new style of teacher. He is totally grounded in spiritual practice and offers you a personal wisdom so that your life might benefit. You do not need to join anything, give up anything other than limiting beliefs, take up any religious practice or adopt a particular lifestyle. What he brings is the revitalizing power of the new idea. So potent is the power of an idea whose time has come that when he spoke on Oprah's show 30 million people tuned in to hear him. His message through the medium of mass communication provides a perfectly framed Aquarian moment: global communication enables a new idea to be disseminated freely to the massed mind. Western teachers appear in unexpected places and guises. Oprah herself has become a true inspiration for so many, women especially. She is a powerful model of personal transformation. Speaking in the language of today she draws upon a wellspring of timeless spiritual wisdom and embodies the possibilities of a transformed life. With some notable exceptions, women have been denied a voice within the oldest traditions. Now, perhaps for the first time, women have become spiritual teachers and will bring a powerful understanding to the newly emerging wisdom stream. It was John Lennon who gave us the phrase, *Power to the People*. How right he was. This has become the time for personal and collective empowerment. The process is ongoing and self-seeding. This is indeed the dawning of the Age of Aquarius whose characteristics are communication, technology, revolutionary ideas and the emergence of the family of humanity. This is the full nature of the revolution in hand.

It is easy to understand the historical and cultural factors that have generated a separated spiritual life in so many places. When the knowledge and peace offered by the monastery or temple was in stark contrast to the ignorance of the outside world and the quiet of the sanctuary was a true retreat from the ravaging desires of war lords, barons and power-hungry rulers, who brought chaos to the kingdom, the split between the two worlds was a daily reality. Although the polarity between war and peace, ignorance and knowledge, chaos and order is still marked around the world, it is no longer the universal pattern. The time of separation has enabled a rich and intense spiritual life to flower in a multitude of guises. The religious traditions of the world have each become rich repositories of human possibilities. The infinite varity of prayer and praise, song and sound, icon and architecture is a bountiful harvest. The mindset of separation, however, is ultimately divisive and sets one path against another in righteous fervour. The mindset of unification brings diverse paths together with respect and in recognition of each other. Separation is now giving way to unity as boundaries dissolve through the medium of communication and exchange. The book, the video and the Internet have opened a doorway into the great religions of past and present. The temple walls have become transparent. The outside world may peer in and the inside world may see outwards. In this new time renouncing the world is no longer essential in order to find the spiritual life. The path to the spiritual life is on your doorstep.

The Whole Life

Walking on water is certainly miraculous, but walking peacefully on earth is an even greater miracle.

John Gray, *Practical Miracles*

Let us celebrate the potency of the time in which we live. As John Gray so rightly says, 'This special time is finally here . ... Humanity has been preparing for this change for thousands of years.' [1] It is here, so how will you respond? Do you believe that this time is in some mysterious way special? Or does your logical mind tell you that, 'Yes sure, every time is special so what is all the fuss about.' Do you look at the suggestion a little incredulously and think, 'Well maybe it's special to him but not to me', or are you really able to embrace the idea as an opportunity given to you? What is preventing you from grabbing the idea with both hands? Will you walk into the future as an Aquarian citizen, conscious of both your place in the world and the spiritual world within your being?

The challenge of our time is integration. The spiritual life was once hidden away, privately led and even secretly protected. Now a different spiritual way is appearing. It is centred wherever you find yourself in life. There is no aspect of life that meditation cannot touch. There is no place where spiritual values cannot operate. There is no part of life that is immune from spiritual insight. Make no mistake – this challenge is monumental. It asks us to move beyond all that we have been brought up to believe. What do you need to be financially successful, happy and healthy? John Gray tells you that, 'To be financially successful, nurture a loving family and sustain a healthy fit body requires a tremendous spiritual grounding'. This is not what you were brought up to believe! These goals are associated with hard work, education, application, even a touch of luck perhaps, but not with 'spiritual grounding'. He says of his own extraordinary life, 'Since I made spirituality my first priority, the rest of my life has flourished.'[2] What is your first priority? Meditation provides the centralizing, underlying bedrock of spiritual practice from which all else will flow.

How is it possible to spiritualize a working life and home life? How is it possible to bring a spiritual dimension to a relationship, to raising children, to sexuality, to health? Only the new idea can enable us to recognize that the ordinary is the extraordinary, the mundane is the sacred, that spirit and matter are indivisible. The New Age slogan 'mind, body and spirit' is a useful shorthand. It reminds us that we now recognise a unity of thought, form and being. It reminds us that we accept connections between the way we use our mind, how we use the body and the choices we make in life. This is a good starting place for a new holistic philosophy. The revolution that is required is one of depth, not of surface change. We need a revolution that heals that which has too long been broken, separated, divided and fractured in us. This is the time to heal, individually and collectively.

This is a vital aspect of the new way. Healing techniques, methods and approaches have blossomed in the West. The emergence of new ways and forms appears endless, yet the need for physical, emotional, mental and spiritual healing is so great. Lives are deeply damaged by a separatist philosophy with all its ramifications. Meditation has an absolutely central role to play in the new healing. It is not possible to give holistic healing unless a spiritual journey is already established. The desire to heal comes from the opening of a higher consciousness and the ability to heal flowers as the self undergoes expansion in consciousness. Receiving holistic healing with understanding and openness provides the optimum place for self-awareness.

Spiritual Intelligence

The heart of the spiritually intelligent self is, ultimately, the quantum vacuum, the ground of being itself. It is a still and changing ground, and the heart knows it is the still and changing heart.
Danah Zohar and Ian Marshall, *Spiritual Intelligence*

In the vortex of the current revolution, normally unrelated areas are finding a common cause at the cutting edge: physics and mysticism, creativity and technology, neurophysiology and psychology and religion and science are all finding unexpected concord. As we move towards a more holistic framework, the hard and fast boundaries that we historically took upon ourselves now appear to be imprisoning rather than useful. New models are free to emerge when the straightjacket of dogmatic thinking and ideological conformity is loosened.

The new concept of Spiritual Intelligence, SQ, has emerged from the holistic marriage of a grounding in the humanities combined with the scientific measure of up-to-date brain research. The result is a new perspective on who we are. The authors, Danah Zohar and Ian Marshall define SQ as, 'the soul's intelligence, it is the intelligence with which we heal ourselves and with which we make ourselves whole'.[3] This new concept is radical. The word 'spiritual' is sometimes conveniently diminished to describe those whimsical attitudes and irrational choices that lead to opting out rather than opting in. But SQ gives us the concept of a practical and internalized working guidance, which is indispensable to our real needs. So how can SQ help us in daily life? When do we draw upon it? According to the authors, 'SQ is our compass "at the edge", life's most challenging existential problems exist outside the expected familiar, outside the given rules, beyond past experience, beyond what we know how to handle... It is the place where we can be at our most creative. SQ, our deep, intuitive sense of meaning and value, is our guide at the edge. We use SQ to reach forward towards the developed persons that we have the potential to be. SQ helps us to outgrow our immediate ego selves and to reach beyond to those deeper layers of potentiality that lie hidden within us.'[4] A person high in SQ is described by the authors as 'a servant leader', a wonderfully paradoxical term that perfectly describes the transformed self. If SQ is defined as 'our ultimate intelligence'[5] do you already have it? Do you want it? How can you develop it? What are you willing to give up to achieve it? It is perhaps salutary to reflect on the notion that the ways and means to develop SQ have always been available under many different guises. Historically, seeking the unconventional, the hidden and the esoteric in times and places geared to but one convention and mode of thought might mean persecution, even death. Today, at last, the ways and means of developing SQ are free to all.

To gauge your existing SQ, ask yourself the following questions.

Do you have:

- The capacity to be actively flexible and spontaneously adaptive?
- A high degree of self-awareness?
- A capacity to face and use suffering?
- A capacity to transcend pain?
- The quality of being inspired by vision and values?
- A reluctance to cause harm?
- A tendency to see the connections between diverse things?
- A marked tendency to ask 'why' or 'what if' questions?
- A faculty for working against convention?

Meditation brings the capacity to be actively flexible and spontaneously adaptive. It creates a high degree of self-awareness. Meditative practice never shys away from the real issues of human suffering but provides ways and means through its lonely labyrinth. Meditation awakens us to the possibility of being inspired by vision and values. It presupposes a reluctance to cause harm and takes us on a journey to a deeper and unified reality where the connections between diverse things become apparent. We are only ready to begin meditation when we are ready to ask fundamental questions. Finally, if we do not possess enough ability to stand out against convention, a safe hobby will claim our attention, while a potent tool for self-transformation will go unnoticed. Meditation has the power to awaken the function of spiritual intelligence from the collective sleep of the conditioned response. So what value is there in seeking and cultivating SQ, the pearl without price? Let the authors tell you. 'High SQ requires us to be deeply honest with ourselves, deeply aware of ourselves. It requires us to face choices and realize that sometimes the right choices are difficult ones. High SQ demands the most intense personal integrity. It demands that we are aware of and live out of, the deep centre of ourselves that transcends all the fragments into which our lives have scattered. It demands that we recollect ourselves, including those parts of ourselves painful or difficult to own. Most of all high SQ demands that we stand open to experience and that we recapture our ability to see life afresh as through the eyes of a child. It demands that we cease to seek refuge in what we know and learn from what we do not know. It demands that we live the question rather than the answer.'[6]

Once awakened, spiritual intelligence takes on a guiding role that directs life choices. This part of ourselves is unfamiliar and so completely different from the normal experience of mind that we experience its eternal wisdom and transcendent authority as belonging to another dimension or realm of being. It is the 'still small voice of calm', the inner guide, the guardian angel or divine presence. Yet this voice is also so deeply familiar that we recognize its truthful resonance in an instant. The first encounter with the indwelling spiritual intelligence is often profoundly moving, possibly even shattering, as the voice of transcendent authority makes itself known. It is the voice of transpersonal knowing or the higher self that is recognized within all spiritual traditions. The indwelling spiritual intelligence cannot be heard or heeded through the clang of conversation, the babble of gossip or the roar of intellectual process. This subtle intelligence requires a quiet mind and a steady focus otherwise its message will be missed altogether. In other words, the practice of meditation awakens the spiritual intelligence and provides space in which its guidance can be maintained. As a dialogue develops between different levels of mind, so Spiritual Intelligence becomes a constant companion and assumes the role of an internal but detached observer of the games we play. The witness within, the watcher on high, brings its own gift of self-awareness, which ultimately effects a total transformation of being. This is the way of the spiritual path.

We do indeed inhabit interesting times. The call to spiritual awakening was once heard only by the few, now it goes out to everyone. If you have heard this inner prompting, however vague and faint, follow your instinct. This is the voice of your own SQ at work. Do not be daunted by the whole picture, which cannot be grasped but simply ask what is the next step for you. Will you close this book and forget or continue on your way. Will the spiritual path enrich and change your life? The gate has never been more widely open, the road ahead never so broad. Now is a good time to begin. You will find yourself in good company. This is the dawning of the Age of Aquarius, when spiritual wisdom becomes possible for everyone. This is the new context in which we now travel.

Astrological insights

A penetrating knowledge of astrology enables a person to better understand his involvement with his family,

friends and co-workers in the light of zodiacal responses
to current cycles of change.

Landis Knight Green, *The Astrologers' Manual*

The symbolism of Aquarius has much to show us. The
astrological sign for Aquarius is drawn as two zig-zag lines,
one above the other. It is the 11th sign of the zodiac and one of
the Air signs. The constellation of Aquarius is depicted as a
kneeling figure carrying an urn upon one shoulder. These
symbols are ancient, but as pertinent as ever. Symbolic
language is never silent, only forgotten when the rational mind
becomes too strident. Symbolic language simply speaks for
itself. The astrological sign for Aquarius, the two zig-zag lines
one above the other, is reminiscent both of water and of
electrical power, which alerts us to technological and
rejuvenating potency of Aquarius. The two lines mirror one
another: 'As Above, so Below,' says the ancient Hermetic
axiom. This ancient clarion still powerfully cries out for a
holistic approach to life. It is a call being answered in so many
ways. As the seasonal markers of solstice and equinox are
increasingly celebrated, the connections between the great
above and the great below are reforged, for it is the heavens
that set the calendar of our lives. When we remember the one
we acknowledge the other. In our times the phrase, 'As Above,
so Below' may carry a new and quite literal meaning. The
damage we have wrought to the ozone layer is reflected here
on earth. Ecological awareness has never been sharper or more
needed. Rediscovering Gaia is a vital thread in the great
seamless garment of the Aquarian current. Casting our full
attention to the earth at our feet is an excellent starting place
for the spiritual journey. The earth is our shared home; we have
no other. Casting our full attention to the heavens is also a
jumping off point for the birth of spiritual awareness.
Contemplating the vastness and infinite majesty of space brings
an awesome reverence for the fullness and complexity of the
greater world in which we travel. As a sign composed of two
parts, Aquarius speaks of both duality and unity. A secular
outer life and a sacred inner life combine to build a rich and
meaningful integrated whole life. There is no longer any need
to choose between either a secular or a sacred path. Both can
now interweave and overlap as part of the one life. Integration
is the way forward. Holism is the new philosophy that speaks
of both unity and diversity, not separation and boundaries.

The constellation of Aquarius is symbolized as a human figure
carrying water. This image encompasses all that it means to be

human. Nakedness strips away all pretension and posturing, all are equal, simply human. As the ruler of the 11th House of the Zodiac, Aquarius brings group activity, shared goals and the essential human endeavours that bring a transpersonal identity and expand our sense of belonging. Aquarian consciousness will lead to a fully integrated sense of humanity as family. This concept is still in its infancy. The naked figure kneels with an urn perched on one shoulder, its contents spill out in a continuous stream from the Above to the Below. What are these waters? The revitalizing waters of life, the renewing currents of a fresh source, the purifying waters of mass baptism, thirst-quenching water for that which is parched, life-giving water for that which is dormant. Cast your mind around. Where do you recognize the rejuvenating effects of a new wave. Perhaps in medicine, areas of health and well-being, perhaps in the appearance of new values in education or business, perhaps in matters of equality in racial and gender issues, perhaps in the appearance of the women's movement, perhaps in the appearance of the men's movement, perhaps in the appearance of New Age networks of holistic counsellors, therapists and spiritual practitioners of every variety and tradition. If you are able to cast your mind back to the very different social and cultural atmosphere of recent decades you will find just how much has been swept away by these incoming waters. Although Aquarius is rich in water symbolism it is one of the Air signs. Air is invisible but everywhere, essential to life and shared by all; it cannot be owned but it can be focused and applied. The element of Air represents the quality of Mind. We are immersed in a revolution of ideas. New influences will be registered mentally as ideas and inspirations. The idea whose time has come has the potential to revolutionize the world as the vision is translated into actuality. The sign of Aquarius is ruled by both Saturn and Uranus, a difficult partnership of total opposites. Saturn imposes limitation, Uranus seeks freedom. Saturn seeks structure, Uranus destroys structure. Saturn establishes boundaries in form, Uranus establishes communication without form. This powerful marriage of opposites is being played out wherever the traditional meets the new, the conservative encounters the radical, the hierarchy faces the chaotic. Saturnian characteristics, including resistance to change, adherence to old values and norms, security of the known, an unwillingness to move on, fear of the new, can only be dissolved from within. These refuges offer the collective bolt hole when the new becomes too rapid or too dramatic, but even these security blankets will fall for the new always supersedes the old. Uranian characteristics have immense potency too. This is the power for forward motion, for invention and discovery, for challenge and radical solution. It is a sign of revolution, not evolution, of upheaval and sudden change, of dramatic shift and revelation. It does not bring comfort or ease, but the spirit of adventure, challenge and excitement. As the higher octave of Mercury representing the rational mind, Uranus represents the largely unexplored potencies of the higher non-rational mind. We have not experienced the impact of either transpersonal mind or radical creativity in society at large, except perhaps through handfuls of artistic genius or spiritual visionaries, but Uranus will bring us the inspired, the wildly exuberant and the magnificent on a grand scale. Uranian energies have already made themselves known through the revolution that we all love, namely the technological revolution. When the technical and the mentally intuitive aspects of Uranus meet, we might expect devices that measure thought patterns and undiscovered brain activity or devices that are controlled and operated by focused thought! Training the mind may become a new discipline and if so, it will incorporate many of the psycho-spiritual techniques developed by the meditative traditions, for this is how the mind is trained and transformed. Here, then, are the Aquarian seeds: the quest for holism, the ecological imperative, the humanitarian impulse, the marriage of secular and sacred, the awakening of the higher mind, mass initiation and grassroots spirituality. You can assist the Aquarian lotus to flower by planting the seed deep in the infinite space of the heart, where it will be nurtured in the mysterious and wonderful setting of your own journey towards wisdom.

introduction

> The gift of learning to meditate is the greatest gift you can give yourself in this life.
>
> Sogyal Rinpoche, *Meditation*

There can be no doubt that interest in meditation continues to grow as ordinary people struggle to make sense of increasingly complex and hectic lives. It is clearer than ever that personal meaning will never be found in the technological accoutrements of contemporary life, no matter how exciting such tools appear to be. Technological mastery is no provider of well-being or peace of mind. Material goods offer a seductive and short-lived satisfaction to those who gain them and serve as a bitter disappointment to those who seek them without success. Technology and materialism are here to stay; these are the driving forces of contemporary society. We cannot change our own history, but we can find a greater vision where these twin powers have a place, but do not rule. When every waking moment has become consumed by consumerism, when the still voice of the heart has been drowned out by imagined glitz and glamour, we have paid too high a price for comfort, ease and security. When the sense of being trapped by the treadmill becomes overwhelming, we know we have failed to strike a healthy balance in our lives. When the relentless passing of time seems to diminish, rather than expand our opportunities for enrichment, who will not cry out, 'There must be more to life than this!'?

In the West, meditation has proved popular as an antidote to our stressful lives. But meditation practice is not simply a remedy for overwork and the ailments of contemporary life. This use is merely an offshoot from a much sturdier tree. Meditation is not relaxation, though it is often confused with it.

Meditation is not therapy, though it has therapeutic applications. Meditation is not an excuse for introspection, but a process of expansion. Meditation is a means of complete personal transformation. Such phrases convey little initially, rather as a description of a foreign and rarely visited land might entice but not really inform the novice traveller. Let the idea become an invitation to initiate your own transformation. Travel yourself and discover the meaning behind the words.

There can be no doubt that meditation originated and flowered in cultures and societies very different from our own. We have little in common with the mountains of Tibet or the monsoon of India. We are worlds apart from the rice fields of Asia and the landscape of Japan. Yet we share a common imperative as human beings, namely to know ourselves. The East has a long and constant meditative tradition. The West has found meditation sporadically. Currently the West is looking to the East as a source of inspiration, while at the same time attempting to develop methods and approaches that suit the circumstances of our lives. We are hoping to draw fresh water from a deep well of ancient wisdom.

Yet we need to remember the very great differences between these two cultures. In the East, where generations of monks have walked and taught, spiritual needs are recognized as legitimate human expressions. The spiritual life is simply integrated into the fabric of life through long established temples, shrines, ashrams and monasteries. There is a sense of balance between the spiritual and the material, the earthly and the eternal. In India, it is acceptable for a man to devote the first half of life to the duties of family in the capacity as householder, but to renounce these same duties and become the spiritual seeker in the second half of life. This acknowledges both the material and spiritual dimensions of life. Moving from the mundane to the spiritual recognizes the healthy mid-life transition. When this is not recognized, it so often afflicts the soul and becomes a mid-life crisis. When mainstream culture sees spiritual commitments as being both normal and real, attending to such needs becomes unremarkable.

In the West, we still nurture a certain suspicion that a sense of spiritual commitment is somehow beyond the norm and not fully real. In the East, the spiritual is honoured by mothers and fathers, grandparents and children. It is part of perfectly normal life. Spiritual expression is simply integral to life. In the West, 'the spiritual' is still treated as something 'other'. Our schismatic mindset is ever operative. Pioneering thinkers, spiritual therapists, travellers, the bold and the insatiably curious have brought meditation to us only by going beyond Western confines, both physical and cultural. Such rich food has been seized upon by the spiritually disenfranchised, the disappointed and the eternally hopeful. Integration is still to come. There can be no doubt that East and West represent two quite different realities by every possible definition. It would not be unfair to note that the East has developed a spiritual life at the expense of the material life, while the West has developed a material life at the expense of the spiritual. Perhaps East and West each has something to give the other.

Who can fail to recognize the spiritual vacuum in our midst? Orthodox religion is fast losing its hold. The whirlpool of change is drawing upon the old and the new, the ancient and the modern, the radical and the traditional. We sense a profound and sometimes frantic attempt to establish a new footing in a rapidly changing world. Activity and massive interest may mask our uncertainty; experimentation has become our hallmark, while the East looks on unruffled.

Meditation beckons us like nourishment to a starving man. It has stood the test of time. We sense our predicament. We recognize the imbalance at the heart of our shared lives. We know that we have served mammon only too well. It is time to redress the balance. It is time to look within. We in the West have lived in the outside world for long enough. Though we may look to the East, it is to ourselves that we must ultimately look. No amount of borrowing or interpretation of ancient texts compensates for a society long divided between the spiritual and the material. Visits by Buddhist Lamas, Zen Roshis and Yogic Gurus serve to remind us of the gaping hole in the fabric of Western culture. As we look towards meditation we come to examine the very values, principles and beliefs that have sustained Western civilization for so long.

Meditation is not a secular activity; we cannot escape this basic fact. Meditation has developed within the broader context of the great spiritual traditions of the world. This does not mean that we should equate meditation with any particular religious belief. We need to make a distinction between the exoteric and the esoteric face of any organized religion. The exoteric body transmits those specialized teachings, codes of behaviour, relevant laws, practices and observances that uphold a particular social, cultural and religious identity. This is the religion of the masses where there is a place for everyone. Within the exoteric religious body there exists an esoteric heart. This is the place of spiritual experience, not social gathering. It is the active path of personal transformation, not the place for handed down dogma. It is the path for the few. The Sufi Way preserves the inner tradition within Islam. *Kabbalah* provides the inner path within Judaism. Christianity has its mystical side too. The many paths of Yoga represent yet another esoteric tradition. Within Buddhism the esoteric and exoteric have not become separate identities but remain intertwined.

While we find great divergence of belief and intent between the religions of the world, we find a remarkable unity throughout the esoteric traditions. We find ourselves standing at the outer door in the hands of our parents. We arrive at the inner door by our own efforts because we have deep and burning questions. We stand with many questions and much confusion. We hold a vague sense of the spiritual. We feel unsatisfied with the answers we have been given throughout life. As we pause at this threshold we may either return or proceed. If we proceed we will find that both responsibility and commitment are placed firmly in our own hands. Self-knowledge and self-awareness lie ahead. Our questions will have a place but the answers will come not from the intellectual and rational mind but from the expanded consciousness, insight and the seeds of wisdom, which are the hallmarks of the meditative mind.

01

beginning: the first step

In this chapter you will learn:
- about the noble eightfold path
- about the eight limbs of Yoga
- about the spiritual path
- about the path of concentration
- the subjects for meditation.

Meditation begins with sila which is virtue or moral purity.
Daniel Goleman, *The Meditative Mind*

Getting ready

It is wisely said that the journey of a thousand miles begins with a single step, so let us begin. Your journey towards meditation will take shape as you find yourself this very day. This path will be built within your life as you find it now. The practice of meditation will arise from your own needs, aspirations and intentions. The life that is yours today is like a seedbed in which you have chosen to plant the possibility of meditation. Your behaviour, attitudes, values and commitment will determine whether this seed dies or flourishes. People come to meditation for many differing reasons. It can begin out of curiosity or as a dimly felt need. It can commence as a purely intellectual interest or an antidote to stress. It is sometimes triggered by a crisis. More often it is the end result of a long process of discontent and dissatisfaction with the goals offered by society. It is possible to be successful, financially independent, surrounded by the trappings of family and career and yet still feel empty. Some people just have an instinctive feeling that there is more to life than just a succession of experiences.

From the outset it should be understood that meditation touches the whole life and the whole person. Therefore the first step towards meditation consists of taking stock of the person we are today, of the life we have today and of the whole situation in which we find ourselves. This is no idle suggestion but a serious request and an opportunity to build your future meditation practice on a firm foundation. Please, take some time for personal reflection. What factors have led you towards meditation? What hopes and expectations do you have? Do you feel ready to plant the seed of meditation in your life? Are you willing to be changed through meditation?

We should not forget that meditation has always been part of a wider spiritual life. Meditation is an integral aspect of all Buddhist and Yogic practice. Taking the practice out of its wider context is not without difficulties. By contrast, meditation remains undeveloped in theory and practice within mainstream Western spirituality. Despite the fact that we find relatively few deep cultural hooks to which we may attach practice, we seek meditation with sincere heart and genuine need. We may profitably look to the older, long established traditions of the

East, while at the same time bearing our own cultural and spiritual circumstances in mind. This particular period offers great opportunities. Meditation is not static, but dynamic. The West has its own needs, and recognizing and meeting our needs may legitimately give rise to new forms of ancient principles. Meditation can take many forms, as history shows. Through time, practice has evolved as enlightened teachers have arisen and nourished the tradition that nourished them. There can be no doubt that meditation is a living stream. The West may drink deeply here too.

It is valuable to understand the origins and developments of the great spiritual traditions of the world. Buddhism, which now has several forms, began with the life of Prince Siddhartha Gautama, son to King Shuddhona and Queen Mahamaya. Wise men were consulted to explain a dream received by the queen. The wise men prophesied that the child Siddhartha could become either a great universal monarch or a great religious teacher. His father, King Shuddhona, determined that his son should pursue the life of the world and so created a fabulous world of pleasure and plenty with which to occupy the prince. Time passed, Siddhartha grew, married and had a son, but he longed to see beyond the palace. Despite every effort, the king could not prevent the curious Siddhartha from seeing the real world. For the first time, Siddhartha encountered death, sickness and old age, and he was deeply moved and shocked. On a fourth outing, Siddhartha met a wandering holy man and saw a new possibility. Though he returned to his palace, his thoughts now turned to leaving the life of plenty. Finally, he left the palace and undertook the great quest. During the next six years he mastered the spiritual practices of his time. He learned concentration and followed the path of extreme asceticism. However, he knew that liberation still eluded him. Determined to find enlightenment he settled into meditation beneath the shade of a tree and with each hour of the night came revelation. By dawn he had attained enlightenment. He knew, 'I have attained the unborn. My liberation is unassailable. This is my last birth. There will now be no more renewal of becoming.' He was transformed from the man, Siddhartha Gautama, to the Buddha, 'One who is Awake.' The prophecy of the wise men was set in motion.

Details of the birth of Patanjali are more mythical than factual. A devout woman, Gonika prayed for a worthy son. At the same time, Adisesa, Lord of Serpents, bearer to the God Vishnu, began to meditate on who would become his earthly mother. In meditation Adisesa saw the figure of Gonika. In her world,

Gonika meditated upon the sun and as she did so a tiny snake emerged on her palm and immediately was transformed into a human who asked to become her son. Gonika was delighted and she named him Patanjali – *pata* means 'fallen' and *anjali* means 'hands folded in prayer'. Even though it has been suggested that the 196 Aphorisms attributed to him are in fact the collected works of more than one author, Patanjali is always referred to as **svayambhu**, an evolved soul who incarnated in order to help humanity. These uncertain details need not detract from the wisdom to be found in the *Yoga Sutras*, which open with a code of conduct and close with a vision of man's true nature.

At this point we may profitably look at the principles that sustain Buddhist and Yogic practice. Both the Noble Eightfold Path of Buddhism and the Eight Limbs of Yoga provide a context in which meditation can take root. If we do not set meditation within the context of a whole life, we make the fundamental mistake of believing that we can simply add practice to daily life without truly making the space to incorporate and integrate its effects. There are some noteworthy similarities between the Noble Eightfold Path and the Eight Limbs. In each case a moral framework precedes meditation practice. Both traditions establish clear moral ground rules that cover behaviour in all forms, social, moral and ethical. Buddhism sets out the Five Precepts, which expressly forbid killing, stealing, sexual misconduct, lying and taking intoxicants. Yoga commences with the Five Yamas, which are non-violence or non-injury, truthfulness, not stealing, chastity and non-acquisitiveness. Both traditions build the practice of meditation upon a period of moral and ethical preparation. A period of preparation has value that should not be overlooked. In our present culture of moral relativism, we are ready to ignore the idea of a preliminary moral training. Yet this always precedes Eastern practice. As a result Westerners are ill prepared for the psychological changes that rightly take place during the period of preparation. Meditation, which is the development of consciousness and the discovery of a deep one-pointed state of mind, can only truly arise from the moral life.

The Noble Eightfold Path of Buddhism

> I take refuge in the Buddha,
> I take refuge in the Dharma,
> I take refuge in the Sangha.
> *Taking Refuge*

- Right understanding: this sets out the first step on the path. It asks us to set out with the right attitude about the journey we have chosen to undertake. Right understanding includes understanding the karmic nature of events and understanding that the true nature is to be found in impermanence.
- Right thought: this stresses the importance of the thoughts that arise in the mind. Right thinking means being aware of desires that arise in the mind.
- Right speech: this covers interactions with others. It includes speaking the truth, avoiding slander, gossip and harsh language. Right speech establishes harmony and peace between people.
- Right action: this restates the moral precepts. It includes not killing, minimising pain to others, not stealing and avoiding sexual misconduct.
- Right mode of livelihood: this covers social and economic relations. Work should not be harmful to others, involve stealing, dishonesty or killing.
- Right effort: this refers to the fact that effort is required by the individual.
- Right intellectual activity: this refers to the mindful use of consciousness.
- Right contemplation: this refers to one-pointedness of mind. It is the ability to stay focused on a subject.

The Eight Limbs of Yoga

> Let us bow before the noblest of sages, Patanjali, who gave Yoga for serenity and sanctity of mind, grammar for clarity and purity of speech, and medicine for perfection of health.
>
> Prayer of Invocation

- Yama – self control or restraints: the five **yamas** are non-violence or non-injury, truthfulness, not stealing, chastity and non-acquisitiveness.
- Niyama – observances: The five **niyamas** are purity, contentment, religious effort, the study of scripture and devotion.
- Asana – posture: **asanas** are familiar to all students of Yoga as the physical poses of the tradition. However, the asana is not merely a physical action but a bridge between mind, body and soul.

- **Pranayama** – breath control: **prana** means life force and **ayama** means ascension, expansion and extension. Pranayama is the application of the controlled breath to the life force.
- **Pratyhara** – sense withdrawal: the work of stilling the five senses builds naturally upon the practices already established and prepares the mind for the practice of meditation.
- **Dharana** – concentration: concentration needs to be developed as a basis for deeper meditation.
- **Dhyana** – meditation: meditation proper flows from the development of concentration.
- Samadhi – contemplative experience: the state of **samadhi** stems from the established meditative mind. It is a state of deeply focused awareness.

These principles provide a solid foundation from which the spiritualized life may arise. Western spirituality does not offer a counterpart. Once again it is worth taking the time to reflect and consider. What characteristics would you consider to be important as a foundation for a spiritually based life? Let there be no mistake – the practice of meditation is derived from the monastery and the ashram. It may have travelled into the outside world with good effect, but it remains the spiritual discipline *par excellence*. We should not make the mistake of attempting to separate the practice of meditation from the life in which it is lived.

The spiritual path

If you wish to know the road up the mountain, you must ask the man who goes back and forth in it.

Japanese proverb

It is common to speak of the spiritual life as a path. This metaphor has value as it gives us the idea of a journey with a beginning and a destination. It is also comforting to realize that we are not alone and that others have trod this same path before us. The idea of the path is established most strongly in the East, where monastic communities have a long history. In such specialized environments a shared language evolved naturally. Generation after generation ensured continuity through lives of study, practice and discussion. The path is a natural consequence of long lived continuity. Buddhism offers the Lam rim, which is the graduated path to enlightenment. Hinduism recognizes diversity in unity and it offers several avenues: the *Karma Marga* is the Path of Action; the *Bhakti Marga* is the devotional path; the *Jhana Marga* is the Path of Knowledge and the *Virakti Marga* is the Path of Renunciation. These various avenues recognize that individuals bring different temperaments to the spiritual life.

By contrast the idea of a path is less developed in Christianity. Christian mystics have indeed existed, but where Eastern mystical experience has successfully evolved into a line of transmission, the Christian mystic has proved to be the exception rather than the rule and, as a result, a lineage of mystical transmission has never evolved.

The concept of the path is not absent from Western esoteric tradition, however. Through the lifelong work of Alice Bailey, a new and extensive corpus of esoteric material was incorporated into the Western heritage. She acted as a telepathic receiver for a figure who chose to be known simply as the Tibetan. In these recent works we find a helpful outline.

The Universal Path

> Nothing can arrest the progress of the human soul on its long pilgrimage from darkness to light from the unreal to the real from death to immortality and from ignorance to wisdom.
>
> Djwahl Khul, *Problems of Humanity*

The Tibetan divides the spiritual path into three stages: the Path of the Probationer, The Path of the Disciple and the Path of the Initiate. The Probationary Path corresponds to the period when the spiritual call has been sensed in some way. It is a time of distinct questing and searching. According to the Tibetan, this period is characterized by self-aware character building, a conscious desire to assist the side of evolution, a rudimentary interest in the Divine Wisdom and a desire to be identified with transpersonal intent. This period of life is outwardly active. Books are avidly read, teachers are sought, groups are joined. It is often a challenging and frustrating period; disappointments go hand in hand with discoveries. However, diligent questing does bring a reward with the seeker finding a spiritual home, which provides support and sustenance. The individual is able to deepen both commitment and understanding. The quest does not cease but expands in scope continuously.

The stage of discipleship, as the name implies, establishes the unshakeable commitment to spiritual principle. However, this too is a time of challenge and personal growth for the doors of spiritual responsibility now open to new horizons. The seeker becomes committed, aspirations begin to change, values shift and priorities are altered. The frenetic activity of the early years is replaced by a more focused but settled outer life. According to the schema written by the Tibetan, the Path of the Disciple is characterized by a deeper commitment to serve humanity and its evolution, the development of the higher faculties of consciousness, a shift from the personal to the transpersonal and a deepening realization of the spiritual responsibilities that come from spiritual awakening.

Finally, the consolidating work of the Path of the Disciple flowers into the Path of Initiation. This is characterized by successively deeper spiritual experiences, a continuous expansion in consciousness and an increased understanding and interaction with the non-physical levels of reality. This brings a total transformation of being at all levels. The path and the individual merge, the initiate takes up the challenges and work of the tradition with fullness and joy.

This outline has universal application: curiosity changes to commitment, spiritual questing brings its reward, consciousness is expanded. Meditation is the single key to the unfolding of this pattern. Without the unifying practice, curiosity will remain idle, questing will be incomplete and consciousness can do no more than process information.

We can begin to unravel the complexities of meditation by drawing upon the familiar image of a target. As a target serves to direct our aim, so the subject of a meditation serves as a target within the mind. Quite simply during meditation, the practitioner will attempt to keep the mind focused on the subject of the meditation. In other words, thoughts will be aimed at a particular target. We find this notion in the Judaic tradition through the classical Rabbinical term for mental concentration, **kavvanah**, which is intentionality. The word is derived from kaven meaning to aim. The development of *kavvanah* is a central theme of the Judaic mystical tradition. It is the same one-pointed concentration elsewhere called *samadhi*. It is the state of higher consciousness. At its simplest meditation may be described as a state of focused awareness.

figure 1.1 meditation places a target in the mind

Focused awareness: the path of concentration

> Although at first our concentration may be very brief, if
> we persevere in the practice it will progressively lengthen.
>
> Geshe Rabten, *Treasury of Dharma*

Using the idea of a target in the mind, it is easy to see that our
intention is to strike as near to the bull's eye as often as possible.
This is, of course, much easier said than done as anyone who
has tried will know. Nevertheless, we should not be
disheartened by early failure. The difficulty of this apparently
simple task has been recognized by the sages and spiritual
teachers of all times. In the *Bhagavad Gita*, Arjuna says, 'The
mind is so relentless, inconsistent. The mind is stubborn, strong
and wilful, as difficult to harness as the wind.' It does not take
long to discover the truth of this statement. Soon enough, we
come face to face with our own mental clutter, our boredom,

our resistance and our inability to concentrate. As we set out on the journey towards meditative practice, it may be that we are considering the qualities of mind for the first time. There is much to discover and much to learn. Geshe Rabten describes meditation as 'a means of controlling, taming and eventually transforming the mind'.[1] This ambitious goal begins in the simplest way; we begin to develop a more focused awareness. This includes a level of sustained concentration and additionally contains an element of self-observation. Using the mind in this way is quite different from everyday awareness, which makes no attempt constantly to review itself. A simple exercise will introduce you to the idea of one part of the mind watching another. Watch the stream of your own consciousness by observing your own thoughts.

EXERCISE 1 JUST WATCHING

Simply sit quietly for a short period of time; no more than a few minutes will be enough. Close your eyes and turn your attention inwards. Try to watch and remember everything that is happening inside your mind. This is more difficult than it sounds. When you have finished, write down all the thoughts that came to you in that short time.

The results are usually surprising: distant memories, associations, future plans and disconnected ideas flow at an extraordinary pace. The idea of slowing down our thinking is a helpful analogy. The first attempts to focus our awareness often prove to be disheartening. Unwanted thoughts arise as if from nowhere. Developing this skill as a sustained and reliable ability will take time and effort. It will not happen in a week, it will not happen without frustration. It will not happen without personal commitment. The advice from the experienced is universally gentle and comforting; don't give up, just carry on. Don't get involved in your thoughts, just let them pass. Return the mind to the subject of the meditation, the target. Allow other thoughts to flow through. Stay focused. Stay aware.

Focused awareness clearly demands a development in concentration. Unfortunately this particular quality still smacks of the classroom and enforced learning, which is not helpful. Too often we associate concentration with mental strain, intense effort and difficulty. Concentration is not an end in itself but the necessary precondition that excludes distractions and diversions. Without concentration no subject for meditation can be held in the mind. Geshe Rabten presents us with six similies of concentration, which enable us to extend the concept of meditative concentration to include qualities of calmness, constancy, dynamism, clarity and lightness. The six similies of concentration are set out below:

1 Concentration is likened to the way a small child views a painting. The child will be aware of the whole canvas but oblivious to the small details. In the first stage we begin to observe the mind at work without the need to observe the fine details of processes.

2 Concentration is likened to the calmness of an ocean that is not disturbed by the individual events taking place in it or upon it. A calm mind should not be disturbed by external events such as a knock at the door.

3 Concentration is likened to the sun shining in a cloudless sky. Mental concentration should be bright and clear, unclouded by dullness.

4 Concentration is likened to the great birds, such as eagles or vultures, in flight. These birds flap their wings briefly and then glide for great distances. The mind should be able to provide short bursts of energy, which then sustain mental flight.

5 Concentration is likened to a bird flying in the sky. It leaves no trail as it passes through the sky. Thoughts come and go but the well-developed concentration is constant.

6 Concentration is likened to a cottonwood seed or piece of down that floats gently on the air. When we meditate we must concentrate in such a way that our mind remains very light, and does not become heavy and tired.

Meditation begins with concentration, the focused awareness. This is the first step but not the last. Concentration requires a subject, the target at which we will take aim.

Subjects for meditation

Everything can be used as an invitation to meditation.
Sogyal Rinpoche, *Meditation*

We do not need to look to the arcane and the distant but to the ordinary and the present for meditation subjects. Meditation is considered to be a means of uncovering the true nature of the human being. Practice therefore often commences with ordinary human activities such as breathing and moving. Awareness is focused on these mundane activities. Daily activities serve as the target for the opening of the meditative mind. The breath is followed universally as a subject for meditation. It is, after all, an obvious and simple choice. Focused awareness becomes mindful as we take in more and more everyday activities. We begin to live mindfully instead of mindlessly as we attempt to notice what we are doing as it happens. So much of daily life is automatic and neglected. Meditation brings awareness into ordinary life.

In complete contrast to the detached observation of natural processes, meditative practice may also focus on created visualized images. This form of meditation draws upon the mind's ability to create and hold internal images. This approach is widely found in Tibetan Buddhism and the Western Mysteries. Such images are invariably symbolic and often complex. A word has a particular limited meaning but a symbol speaks volumes. It opens the mind through a rich train of associations and connections. Meditation can take place on a single symbol or a constellation of symbolic images. The symbolic offers a rich vein for meditative and contemplative thought. Symbols serve to expand consciousness and develop the qualities of insight and intuition. Symbols can be presented for meditation through innumerable forms. Sometimes a physical representation is used, at other times the image is just created with one part of the mind while it is simultaneously

figure 1.2 this simple mandala shows the basic structure of the typical Tibetan mandala

contemplated. Symbolic paintings, constructions, stories, statues, sacred objects, treasured icons and even imagined realities all serve to transform the mind.

Particular symbolic traditions have evolved as certain forms have become regularly employed. The **mandala** is a circular symbolic representation of both universal and personal forces. It is employed in a particular way for meditation. The traditional Tibetan mandala is drawn according to a symbolic schema and approached through a long established convention.

The **yantra** is another visual representation but it uses geometric shapes to represent cosmic and personal connections. The *Shri Yantra* is composed of nine interpenetrating triangles, which symbolize male and female energies. It represents the whole of creation.

The Judaic mystical tradition is unique in representing a complex philosophy entirely in symbolic form. This is a most remarkable interplay between philosophy and symbol. The single embracing image, **Otz Chiim** or the Tree of Life, contains

figure 1.3   the *Shri Yantra*

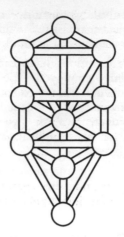

figure 1.4 *Otz Chiim* – the Tree of Life

a host of interconnected symbols. Here is a lifetime's study and meditation.

Subjects for meditation are varied and endless, traditional and emergent, widely different yet unified in purpose. In startling contrast to the symbolic and the ordinary, Zen Buddhism holds a unique place among meditative traditions. It takes no subject as its subject and rejects all conceptual tools, words, images, theories and mental structures. It has created its own unique series of subjects for meditation, namely the **koan**, a riddle without an answer. As we consider meditation practice in further detail, we can remain open to endless possibilities.

Although certain subjects have become traditional through extended use, we should not feel confined by the past or intimidated by the learned. Sogyal Rinpoche takes meditation right into the heart of daily life. He reminds us to be inventive, resourceful and joyful as we take the openness of the meditative mind into the everyday world: 'A smile, a face in the subway, the sight of a small flower growing in the crack of a cement pavement, a fall of rich cloth in a shop window, the way the sun lights up flower pots on a window sill. Offer up every joy, be awake at all moments.'[2] Subjects for meditation are everywhere.

Joining the company

Close your eyes for a moment and imagine that you are standing beside a broad pathway. People are walking along. Some walk in groups, others travel by themselves. You stand and watch them pass. You notice that these people radiate a serenity and contentment that you have only rarely seen. Someone comes over to you and offers you a warm handshake.

'Are you coming?'
You reply and ask, 'What will I need to take with me?'
    'Everything that you are.'
    'Where are we going?' you ask.
    'To discover all that you can be', comes the reply.
    'When shall we start?' you ask.
    'Right now.'

You step onto the path and people greet you with warm smiles, knowing that you have just joined them. Your journey has begun.

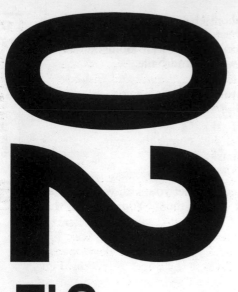

02

opening: the inner frontiers

In this chapter you will learn:
- about the cycle of meditation
- practical preparation for meditation
- how to keep a meditation journal.

Meditation means many things: it means turning inwards; it means quiet observation, reflection and awareness of ourselves; it means to be conscious of consciousness, to become a detached observer of the stream of changing thoughts, feelings, drives and visions, until we recognize their nature and their origins.

Lama Govinda, *Creative Meditation*

East and West

As we open ourselves to the possibility of meditation, we naturally look to a frame of reference in which we can place ourselves. Bearing this in mind we can look briefly at meditation in the East and the West. There are certain clear differences in the metaphysical underpinning of East and West. The West has revolved around a theistic model. The East has developed a spiritual richness without always invoking a personified godhead. Life in the West has turned towards the world. Life in the East has turned away from the world. Owing to our political and religious background, the esoteric path has remained a constant but hidden way. In such circumstances the Western mystical lineage has been narrow. It is not insignificant that the Western mystical tradition is enshrined in a symbolic vocabulary, which has served to protect and veil mystical experience from unwelcome gaze. Historically, the cultural and political conditions of the East permitted the emergence of many a spiritual lineage. The West has only recently developed a means of enquiring into the nature of being and becoming. Psychology has become our avenue for exploration. It likes to keep a healthy distance from anything metaphysical. The East has its psychology too, but it exists in seamless proximity with spiritual method. The two levels of experience are not seen as separate, but as belonging together. Just as the techniques of psychology work within the personal realm, so there is a good case for regarding spiritual exercise, most especially meditation, as a means for transpersonal growth.

In the West very little value has been placed on the subjective life of dream or imagination. In the twentieth century it was the work of Carl Jung that succeeded in refocusing our attention towards the inner world of the psyche. By closely following his own inner life in dreams, vision and meditations, Jung charted an extraordinary domain. This was a major revelation in Western thinking. This inner realm, however, was not unknown by the

East. Western meditative developments have drawn deeply on Jung's work. Much use has been made of the creative or active imagination and here lies a basic difference between the two approaches. Eastern meditation does not seek to explore or enter the life of the mind, but instead seeks to rise above content and reach a level of transcendence. This goal may not be suited to the Western mind, which is still in the throes of discovering the inner life.

As we open ourselves to meditation, the difference in fundamental cultural background needs to be recognized. As individuals we cannot shake off our cultural conditioning as easily as we might like or hope. Several research studies have found that Eastern and Western students respond differently to classical techniques.[1] Having neglected the realm of the subjective for so long, Western students appeared to become fixated on the content of the interior world. Basic meditation training resulted in increased fantasy, daydreaming, reverie, imagery and some spontaneous recall of past memories as depressional or conflict material. A second study by Engler and Brown found that Western students became preoccupied, even fascinated, with images, memories and inner sensations.[2] This fascination may well reflect our deep surprise at discovering the inner world. Dwelling on content in this way is a recognized but temporary stage. When the Eastern student is ready to move on to bypass mental content, a Western counterpart is less willing to do so. It is noteworthy that the eyelids are lowered but not closed in most Eastern meditations. This prevents imagery from arising. By contrast, in the West the eyes are most often closed, which encourages the creation of images. Although some Eastern practices do employ the creative imagination, Western practice rarely seeks to empty the mind. In their study, Brown and Engler asked an Asian Buddhist teacher why Western students are slower to reach more advanced stages of meditation. He replied, 'Many Westerners do not meditate, they do therapy. They do not go deep with mindfulness.' It may be necessary for Western students to spend longer immersed in content rather than process, for we have spent so long denied of both. As the authors of the research comment when speaking of the situation in the USA, 'In this country meditation is indeed a form of therapy for many.'[3] Perhaps that is just what we need.

Let us begin with a model that will serve us as we journey into meditation.

The Cycle of Meditation

The Cycle of Meditation enables us to view meditation as a continuous and dynamic process. Meditation is a process, not an isolated event.

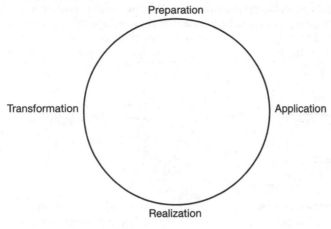

figure 2.1   the Cycle of Meditation

Preparation

Posture

Sit, then as if you were a mountain with all the unshakeable, steadfast majesty of a mountain.

Sogyal Rinpoche, *Meditation*

Meditation begins with sitting. It is common to think that meditation begins with relaxation. But it is important not to confuse the two states. Entering relaxation serves more as a demarcation between the outer busy world and the inner state that we are seeking. Although it is not uncommon to formally relax as preparation for meditation, this stage should eventually be dispensed with so that meditation can be entered directly.

There is no doubt that the full lotus position is still favoured by the classical meditative traditions. In this position the foot of the right leg is placed over the left thigh and the foot of the left leg is placed over the right thigh. However, this is a difficult position for most people. Less strenuous variations are possible, but these also require a level of suppleness, which may well prove too difficult. In the half-lotus position, one foot lies on the opposite thigh while the other foot rests under the opposite thigh. In the quarter-lotus position, while one foot lies under the opposite thigh, the remaining foot lies under the opposite leg. All these crossed-leg postures present difficulties for many Westerners; we are just not used to sitting in this way. It is of course possible to work towards these positions if you choose, but daily work on the muscles of the thighs and legs, ankle joints and feet are required. If these classical positions are beyond you, take heart that other much easier positions are also suitable. In the traditional Japanese kneeling posture, a cushion relieves pressure on the heels. This kneeling position can also be used on a low bench with padded seat. In Western groups it is common practice to adopt the 'Egyptian pose'. This entails sitting on a hard-backed chair with the feet firmly placed on the floor. Although no single posture is essential for meditative practice, it is universally agreed that the spine should be held upright at all times. No matter which pose is preferred, the intention is to create a stable and balanced position that can be held for periods of quiet.

As meditation becomes integrated into your life, however, you will find that meditation just takes place wherever you are and sitting becomes a matter of choice.

In Buddhist groups it is usual to place the hands in the lap just in front of the navel. The palms are held facing up, the left slightly cupped in the right. The thumbs are held horizontally so that the tips lightly touch. Roshi Philip Kapleau reminds us that by placing the left hand over right, we suppress the active pole of the body in order to bring about a passive tranquillity. The position of the hands is, however, another variable. Geshe Rabten suggests a slight arching of the thumbs so that a triangle is formed with the palms. A quite different approach is used in Yogic groups where the hands are placed on the knees using either the *jnana mudra* or *chin mudra*. In the *jnana mudra* the index finger of each hand is bent so that it touches the inside of the root of the thumb. The remaining three fingers are kept straight. The hands are placed on the knees with the palms turned down and the three straight fingers pointing at the floor in front of the feet. In *chin mudra* the hands face upwards.

Breathing
The process of breathing, if fully understood and experienced in its profound significance, could teach us more than all the philosophies of the world.

Lama Govinda, *Creative Meditation*

figure 2.2 several postures are traditionally adopted for meditation

The nature of the respiratory cycle makes it an ideal subject for the meditating mind. The meditator is only as far away from meditation as the next breath. The cycle is clearly automatic, yet it remains open to a fuller and more conscious participation. Its active and passive phases can be altered within limits by conscious intervention. Yogic practices tend towards intervention, Buddhist practices tend towards participation. Awareness of the breath is a universal meditative practice. It is most often the starting place for meditation. Yet this simplest of subjects may prove to be the most complex. It has been suggested that it is possible to reach enlightenment through awareness of the breath alone.

During meditation, breathing takes place through the nose. This permits a deep abdominal breath. The respiratory cycle is controlled by nerve cells in the brain. The respiratory centre in the *medulla oblongata* is concerned with inspiration and the pneumotaxic centre controls exhalation. Nerve impulses from the respiratory centre are passed directly to the diaphragm. As the diaphragm forms both the floor of the upper thoracic cavity and the ceiling of the abdominal cavity, any change in the upper body is reflected by a change in the lower body and vice versa. As the upper thoracic cavity is expanded, the abdominal cavity reduces and as the thoracic cavity reduces, the abdominal cavity is expanded. The cycle of breathing brings a continuous interplay of expansion and contraction in lungs, diaphragm and abdomen. In meditation, breathe in with a long and deep inhalation. The diaphragm will descend and push out the abdomen slightly. On the outbreath, the diaphragm will rise and flatten the abdomen. You can feel this for yourself by placing a hand on the abdomen. Although it is usual to think of the breath as a twofold cycle, the conscious meditative breath cycle has four components – the inhalation, a pause, the exhalation and a second pause. Any of these four aspects of the breath may be stressed with more complicated techniques.

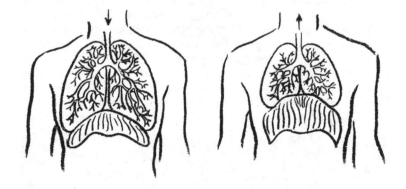

figure 2.3   the meditative breath

During meditation, breathing is conscious rather than automatic; this awareness underpins all meditations. Even though awareness is focused on the breath, random thoughts will continue to arise naturally. When this happens the advice is always to allow such thoughts to pass through, neither following them nor controlling them. Awareness of the breath most often begins with breath counting. This practice also has variations, which range from the basic to the complex. The following four stages are the most commonly used. You can attempt each of these approaches in turn:

1 On the inhalation, count the odd numbers 1, 3, 5, 7, 9, 1 and so on.
2 On the exhalation, count the even numbers 2, 4, 6, 8, 10, 2 and so on.
3 Count each cycle of inhalation–exhalation as one unit. Tally the breath on the exhalation.
4 Count each cycle of inhalation–exhalation as one unit. Tally the breath on the inhalation.

EXERCISE 2 THE BREATH OF LIFE

Choose one of the breath-counting exercises and take this as your meditation for a week.

Following the breath

A more complicated Buddhist technique is described by Geshe Rabten, who explains how mental awareness is used to follow the breath. This involves mentally watching as breaths are drawn into and expelled from the body with increasing depth and distance. In the first stage, the mind follows the inhalation until the inbreath reaches the level of the neck. On the exhalation, the mind follows the outbreath to a point just beyond the nostrils. In the next stage, the mind follows the inhalation into the level of the chest. Likewise, on the exhalation, the mind follows the outbreath the equivalent distance beyond the nostrils. Next, the mind follows the inhalation down to the knees and then follows the exhalation to a corresponding distance from the body. Finally, the mind follows the inhalation down into the feet, then follows the exhalation out from nostrils at a corresponding distance. Placing the breath into the body in this way is of course also a mental exercise. Geshe Rabten states that, 'By doing this exercise, one gains control of the breath and the mind'.[4] In further refinements, the mind is used to analyse and investigate the nature of the air being breathed.

Lama Govinda makes a high claim for breathing, a natural activity that we take for granted. He describes breathing as 'the most sublime function of our organism'. It is a vehicle for spiritual experience: 'It is the mediator between mind and body, it is the first step towards the transformation of the body from a more or less passively and unconsciously functioning organ into a vehicle or tool of a perfectly developed and enlightened mind.'[5] As we become conscious of our own breathing, we find physical calmness and mental quiet. As we turn our awareness increasingly towards the breath, we begin to extend our inner awareness. Additionally, the delicate relationship between the breath and the energies of the subtle bodies will become increasingly apparent as the links between mind and body are developed specifically through **pranayama**, which is the science of the breath.

Pranayama

Pranayama offers a wide variety of techniques for unifying mind and body. The most famous of these is probably alternate nostril breathing, though there are many other specific exercises in combined mind and breath control. Pranayama raises the natural relationship between the breath and the subtle energies to a high art. It has moved far beyond mere observation into control and fully conscious manipulation. The length of both the inhalation and exhalation and the moments between the inbreath and outbreath are each variously emphasized to create a range of breathing callisthenics. The Buddhist way is merely to count, to watch and to become aware of the breath, but the Yogic way is to control, to intervene and manipulate.

Application: the subject of the meditation

> If we do not control the mind, we will achieve nothing.
> Geshe Rabten, *Treasury of Dharma*

After the stage of preparation is complete, the subject of the meditation is brought to mind. This is our target. Whether the subject is our own breath, a symbol, a phrase or an idea, our intention is to return to it over and over again. Although the mind will still wander, the target serves to keep us focused. The process of learning to stay on target requires patience and perseverance. It fosters the development of mental awareness and leads to mental self-control.

Realization – the fruit of the meditation

> Many have come to realization simply by listening to the tinkling of a bell or some other sound.
> Roshi Philip Kapleau, *The Three Pillars of Zen*

Every meditation is like a seed planted in the mind. In time it will bring forth its own fruit. Nothing particular may be apparent on the surface after each meditation but something imperceptible has taken place. The fruit of the meditation is the gain, the realization, the distilled nectar. It is the essence of our inner work and the culmination of our efforts. It may take many forms. There may be a changed conscious understanding or a realization about your own life in general. The culminating realization may come as a dream, in a moment of sudden insight or through a symbol revealed to the inner eye. It may come as a thought or as a non-thought, as a feeling or as a knowing. Be open to all possibilities in yourself. Be aware and you will see the fruit of the meditation ripening. You may even catch it as it falls.

Transformation: the effect of the process

> The faculty of continual transformation ... is a profound expression of the dynamic character of the mind.
>
> Lama Govinda, *Creative Meditation*

This aspect of the process is less easy to identify on a day-to-day basis. We tend not to see ourselves changing, others may see it first. Personal change can sometimes be dramatic but it is most often gradual and organic. This is the most reliable and best way. All too often people come to meditation with unfounded expectations. They hope for the dramatic, the bizarre and the extraordinary. This will not happen. 'The real miracle,' as Sogyal Rinpoche points out, 'is more ordinary and much more useful. It is a subtle transformation and this transformation happens not only in your mind and your emotions but also actually in your body.'[6] Meditation works at a very deep and potent level. It is working even when we do not see anything happening. Once the process has commenced it is self-sustaining. It works much like the body's own natural processes. Body cells are renewed constantly, yet we see no change. The body is transformed continuously by day and by night. Meditation enables us to experience a total transformation gently and quietly from within the depths of being. So if you take up meditation with a good heart and sincere intent, expect to be changed.

Meditation: the way of change

It is not easy for us to change. But it is possible and it is our glory as human beings.

M. Scott-Peck, *The Different Drum*

Change follows regular meditation as surely as night follows day. So do not be surprised when change begins to happen for you. It is impossible to look ahead and see how meditation will work for you. It works at so many levels simultaneously. Meditation brings physical, emotional and intellectual changes, which can culminate in a deep and lasting change that might well be termed a spiritual awakening. The degree to which you will be changed by meditation depends on many factors, including your own need for change. Only you can decide what you need from practice and how much time you will give to it. At the outset, be prepared to be changed as you journey.

Meditation and physiology

Meditation is commonly promoted as an antidote to stress. Nowadays this idea is accepted and acceptable but this was not always the case – this notion was once quite radical. It was during the 1970s that scientific method was first applied to meditation. Research discovered that meditation produced observable physical changes in a number of parameters. It was observed that meditation effected a lowered metabolic rate, which uses less oxygen and produces less carbon dioxide. The lactate concentration of the blood was noted to be decreased during meditation. This was a significant finding as blood lactate level is related to anxiety and tension. Another significant discovery was the noted correlation between meditation practice and specific brainwave patterns. There were some spectacular encounters with yogis and experienced meditators, which showed that consciousness outstripped our ability to measure it. The book *The Relaxation Response*, published by Herbert Benson in 1975, highlighted the therapeutic benefits of the deeply relaxed state. This discovery spawned new approaches in mental and physical treatment programmes. Relaxation began to be used to good effect with patients suffering from high blood pressure and stress-related disorders. Research continued into the 1980s and, in 1984, the National Institute of Health released a consensus report that recommended meditation along with salt and dietary restrictions above prescription drugs as the first treatment for mild hypertension. Researchers found that meditation decreased the body's response to norepinephrine, a hormone indicated in cardiovascular stress. Relaxation has been found to help conditions of angina and arrythmia and to assist in the lowering of blood cholesterol levels. There is still much to learn about the body/mind. The West has compiled 20 years of research, which is very little when set against the accumulated centuries of quiet Eastern practice. Yet the research is already enough to prove that meditation produces observable physical results. No doubt future research, will expand our knowledge. New lines of research may take us deeper into the relationship between the brain and particular forms of mental activity. Though physical results can be beneficial, if we see meditation as an antidote to stress we remain closed to the Eastern view that meditation is the means of spiritual transformation and the path to enlightenment.

Meditation and spirituality

Although we are content to accept meditation practice in the context of physical and even emotional well-being, we are more cautious when meditation refers directly to spiritual transformation. This concept is unfamiliar. Yet in truth this lies at the heart of practice.

Meditation works directly with consciousness. In doing this, we are inevitably taken into the fundamental area of human existence. We work directly with the mind from within. We step into the alchemical furnace of becoming. We come to work with ourselves in depth and finally we come fully to realize ourselves. This sharpens the spiritual quest, which is not undertaken as some vague existential adventure, but under a directive to know ultimate nature. On the journey into the nature of being human, much will transpire.

The quest for human potential is not entirely unrecognized in the West. Transpersonal psychology has emerged as a new and tender shoot from the more established field of humanistic psychology. The first issue of the *Journal of Transpersonal Psychology* in 1969 expressed its concerns as: 'Ultimate values, unitive consciousness, peak experiences, ecstasy, mystical experience, awe, wonder, being, self-actualization, essence, bliss, wonder, ultimate meaning, transcendence of the self, spirit, oneness, cosmic awarenes, related concepts, experiences and activities.' This is the shared ground of East and West. Some have called this quest the search for God, others have termed it the quest for Ultimate Reality. It is undoubtedly a quest that can only be personally undertaken from deep within consciousness itself. As we journey into meditation there is much to discover. We will take from practice what we need, whether it is the antidote to stress or the means to spiritual awakening.

The meditation journal

Newcomers to meditation are most likely to work alone. It is very easy to feel isolated and uncertain. In the Western tradition, it is common for students to keep a personal meditation diary. Perhaps this stems in part from the historical precedent found in the Judaic tradition where the practice of diary keeping has long been advised. Rabbi Joseph Karo, a sixteenth-century mystic, kept a diary for more than 30 years. His contemporary Rabbi Chaim Vital kept a detailed dream diary. *The Midrash* relates that the patriarch Jacob kept a log of significant events, including the dreams of his son Joseph. This is a helpful practice, most especially to newcomers.

Begin your journal with all the things that you hope meditation might help you find. This initial list will help to establish your starting point. In the future you can look back to see how far your experience measured up to your expectations. You may also discover that your expectations themselves changed through your experience. In any event, your first thoughts about meditation are of personal value, so record them. Journal keeping encourages self-discipline and strengthens personal commitment. However, the journal is not the place for lengthy introspection, but for brief and succinct reports, which attempt to distil every practice to its essence. Get into the habit of writing your notes immediately after the session while the ideas are fresh in your mind. The following example might be helpful.

Date: 3 April 1997
Time: 7.00–7.15 a.m.
Meditation subject: counting the breath
Realizations: paid attention to breathing – established deep and regular rhythm. Began to count. Some boredom and a certain irritation with myself – lost my place several times.

Difficulties: distracted by intruding thoughts of what I needed to do later in the day – found it hard to remain in the present moment and to stay with the task in hand. Kept bringing myself back to the count.

There is no time to begin like the present, so make a start today. The inner frontier awaits you.

03 establishing: the integrated life

I cannot say it strongly enough: to integrate meditation in action is the whole ground and point and purpose of meditation.

Sogyal Rinpoche, *Meditation*

The spiritual life

For too long the word 'spiritual' has carried certain connotations of unworldliness. It is easy to think of a monk or nun, guru or priest in this context. These figures represent a withdrawal or renunciation of the world, which marks the dividing line between the householder and the holy man. We should stop and ask ourselves, why is this? The word holy means whole, how may we be holy when we affirm separation through word and deed? Why does it somehow seem less easy to think of an executive or a housewife, a hairdresser or an office worker in a spiritual context? Every seed bears its fruit and we see the result of this idea in the world we have created. Look at the world we have built. Do you see the holy, the whole in the world or do you believe that you must seek it in some far away distant place? Do you think that the holy, the spiritual is hiding from you? Where could it be hiding? Who could be hiding the infinite from you? If it is not in hiding, perhaps it has been here all the time hiding in every cell of matter that already surrounds you. Perhaps you have hidden the spiritual for yourself by banishing it to a remote, inaccessible region. The secular and the spiritual have been divided. Let the secular and spiritual be reunited. The spiritual life is life itself; what else could it be? The spiritual life is not an escape from mundane life, but a transformation of it.

The divide between what is perceived to be spiritual and what is perceived to be material is deeply rooted in Western culture. This stilted theology has run its course. It has taken a heavy toll in the oppression of the human spirit. The notion of separation has become so culturally ingrained as to be invisible, but we feel its effects. We sense the sterility of a life cut off from nature, we feel a sense of intangible loss and we simply realize that something is out of balance in our lives as individuals and in the wider group. Eastern philosophies have never lost a sense of holism. The flesh and the spirit, the world and the divine, manifestation and the Absolute have never become estranged any more than two sides of the same coin. If we keep the mundane and the holy apart, we are merely perpetuating an idea that has served its time. The new frontiers of physics show us more clearly than ever that the manifestation of life is baffling, mysterious and amazing. Matter holds many secrets. We are now searching for holism with all the appetite of a starving person seeking food. There is currently an instinctive desire to reunite body and spirit, heart and mind, the mundane and the supramundane. We are now looking for the very bridges, whether symbolic, psychic or practical, which were severed in the attempt to isolate the spiritual from life itself. Meditation constitutes such a bridge. It resolves the polarities that appear to be separate and reconciles the paradoxes that life presents. We are immersed in the paradoxical, the great and the small, the incomparably vast and the impossibly tiny, natural beauty, human cruelty, human courage, natural disaster, the timeless and the passing of time, human birth, human death and all that passes in between. The resolution of such oppositions has always been the domain of the transcendent, which alone can reconcile such opposing polarities. Matter and spirit, flesh and mind, heart and soul can all be integrated through consciousness.

A narrow definition of the spiritual life fosters a narrowness of outlook, expectation, hope and aspirations. So let us seek a broad definition, which enables us to reach out and embrace life with an open heart. The Lucis Trust offers us the words of the Tibetan. Here is a broad and encompassing definition that can inspire and uplift:

> The word 'spiritual' relates to attitudes, to relationships, and to the moving forward from one level of consciousness to the next. It is related to the power to see a new vision and new and better possibilities. It refers to every effect of the evolutionary process as it drives a man forwards from one range of sensitivity to another; it relates to expansion of consciousness, to all activity which leads towards some further development. The discoveries of science, or the production of some great work in literature or in the field of art, are just as much evidence of spiritual unfoldment as the experiences of the mystic or the registration of any disciple of a contact with his own soul.[1]

In the light of this broad definition, let us move forwards towards a deeper understanding of meditation.

Illusion and reality

> Meditation offers an alternative to the purely materialistic values of modern life, it is a means of harmonizing or resolving the apparent conflict between the spiritual and the material aspects of living.
>
> The Tibetan, *The Science of Meditation*

Scientists describe the world in a particular way, sociologists in quite another, while artists give us another perspective altogether. Curiously enough, we have little difficulty in holding a consensus view. The world is solid enough for us to believe in! Physicists, however, have proof to the contrary. The five senses daily reveal a world of three dimensions, of sound, of taste and colour, of immeasurable sensation. The five senses can reveal nothing about the world of atoms, electrons and particles, yet this is the very stuff of the world we daily inhabit. It takes a powerful microscope to see the minute world of microscopic organisms. It takes a sophisticated telescope to observe the distant reaches of the galaxy. It takes a vast device to capture the mysterious subatomic world of particles. The five senses provide only a very limited view of the world in which we live. Yet we are, for the most part, content to construct a complete personal edifice upon this most limited foundation. So where and what is reality?

Spiritual traditions have always spoken of ultimate reality. Monotheistic religions refer to this as God. Non-theistic paths refer to this as the Absolute. It cannot be fathomed by the five senses or the intellectual mind; it can only be experienced by another level of mind altogether. Meditative practice gives birth to this higher, non-discursive mind. Meditation is the great awakener, the shatterer of illusions. The shift from the concrete and rational mind to the abstract meditative mind can either be precipitated gradually or suddenly. The gradual approach is favoured by most Buddhist approaches and also by *Kabbalah*. The mind is slowly transformed through graduated practice. By contrast Zen seeks a direct and unique approach to the question of human illusions.

We carry our projections into life like a snail in a shell. We become so comfortable with our own world-view that we do not notice how it operates. Let us imagine that three people go into a beautiful garden on a warm summer day. They sit together on a bench. The first person is clearly delighted by the opportunity to sit and enjoy the sun, the view and the quiet. The second person begins to sneeze, while the third begins to extol the medicinal virtues of the varied plants. Quite simply, where is the garden? It exists quite differently for the keen herbalist, the hay fever sufferer and the person who just wants to relax.

Although we may not realize it, we approach so many experiences through the lens of our pre-existing mindset. Reflect for a moment on the freshness and spontaneity that a child finds in everyday experiences. The child is almost surprised daily at the simple delights of ordinary things. The adult so often loses touch with the sense of wonder and curiosity, which makes the world a remarkable and living place. A child's openness to experience is very close to the meditative mind. The child relates directly and without preconceptions to all experience. The processes of socialization and education shape behaviour and reactions into accepted norms. Something is gained, but something is lost along the way. It is perhaps ironic that we have to work so hard to find our way back to the simplicity of childlike consciousness. The educated mind has learned to think in particular and specialized ways, to think rationally and to provide solutions logically. The socialized individual has learned to respond in socially acceptable ways, to adopt the language and manners of the social group and to function within prescribed parameters. Meditation begins where education and socialization finish.

All meditative systems promote self-awareness and detached observation as a means of watching our inbuilt preconceptions and value judgements. Zen simply asks us to see the 'isness' of things, in other words to see things as they are without the added gloss of our own projected imaginings. This seems absurdly simple. The contemporary teacher Osho gives simple advice:

> You look at a flower – you simply look. Don't say 'beautiful', 'ugly'. Don't say anything. Don't bring in words, don't verbalize. Simply look. In the beginning it will be difficult but start with things with which you are not too involved – look at things which are neutral – a rock, a flower, a tree, the sun rising, a bird in flight, a cloud moving in the sky. Start from neutral things and only then move towards emotionally loaded situations.[2]

The Zen Master Sheng Yen made the same point while leading a retreat for a number of students in Wales. Life on the farm was very ordinary. Every day the sheep were herded back into their pens. It was a noisy and distracting experience. But Master Sheng Yen saw the commotion as yet another opportunity to practise awareness. He said the following: 'Every day we hear the baaing of sheep and the bleating of lambs. When the animals are in the yard, there is indeed a great noise. If you are truly practising, you witness the sound and nothing more.'[3] In other words, there was no cause for distraction, merely an experience to be registered and integrated. Seeing things as they are is the simplest instruction and the most complicated task. It is the foundation stone of Zen.

EXERCISE 3.1 SEEING THINGS AS THEY ARE

Attempt to apply this principle as you go about your daily life. Be aware of how you use language to elaborate and embellish. Instead, try just to see directly without enhancement, partiality or sheer invention.

When we only see the world through a lens of our own making, we build a false reality layer upon layer. A news item provides an example. A woman looked out from her window in the early evening and saw a black bear caught high up in a tree. She immediately fetched her neighbour. They both watched for a while but the bear made no effort to move either upwards or climb down. Quite soon a small crowd had gathered and they wondered how best to coax the bear down. The local vet was finally called out to administer an anaesthetizing dart. The local fire brigade made ready to catch the creature as it fell. But despite the dart, it did not fall. Several hours had passed since the bear was first spotted. It was finally decided that the situation called for a desperate measure. The local loggers were summoned and they proceeded to saw away at the tree. Despite all the noise, commotion and activity the bear had remained firmly rooted to its perch. However, as the tree crashed to the ground a black bin liner, fully inflated and tied, floated gently down to the earth. In this case the good folk of the town saw the errors of their shared perception rather quickly and no doubt all felt suitably foolish. However, in life we are rarely so rudely awakened from our dream. In fact, we do a great deal both consciously and unconsciously to preserve our own status quo.

Denial, deception and delusion

If I ignore it, maybe the problem will go away.

Everyday thought

Denial, deception and delusion are everyday realities to the therapist. This is the baggage that we accrue as we travel through life. The longer we carry these three inner demons, the heavier our burden becomes and ridding ourselves of them becomes increasingly difficult. Therapy is a common route. The therapist acts in the capacity of a detached witness by holding up a mirror to our behaviour. Meditation is a less common route. Through meditation we can learn to function in the capacity of a detached observer and hold up a mirror to our own behaviour. In doing this we take an important step towards weaving spiritual values and the ordinary life into one seamless garment.

Without some degree of conscious awareness we remain prisoners of early conditioning and upbringing. We carry behaviours and ingrained responses into later life like invisible millstones. In the interchange of close relationships, we approach every encounter with an array of complex predispositions and long-standing ways of behaving. These personal patterns are the hardest to identify as they have become invisibly embedded within us. Yet like ruts in a riverbed our long established expectations determine reactions and responses. We experience the moments of everyday life through the lens of our own construction. If we have low self-esteem we may feel constantly criticized, and if we are deeply fearful, we cannot trust. If we are lacking in confidence, we may compensate by exuding an air of bravado. Self-justification, passing responsibility and blaming others all permit us to use denial in our own defence. We can deny the big faults and the small faults, we can deny cause and effect, we can deny responsibilities and involvement. The awakened meditative mind, however, permits no such denials, for in the clear light of day self cannot hide from self. Denial will thrive wherever the status quo carries weight. We avoid seeing things as they are and warp the turn of events to maintain the illusion that favours our perspective. We scapegoat others to safeguard ourselves. Though we recognize the truth at some deep hidden level, the truth may be too hurtful to acknowledge openly. Difficult relationships breed self-deception as blame is thrown back and forth. We hide from the truth to protect an image we hold of ourselves. Delusion, denial and deception are the common currency of everyday life and relationships. When we are ready to admit the light of awareness, we are ready to find ourselves.

The way in which we view the world and our place within it shapes our attitudes, intentions and behaviour. A narrow view breeds narrow responses. Viewing the world through the porthole of restricted vision reduces everything to the same scale. A small world-view creates a small world. Every new opportunity, which might bring expansion is rejected, ignored or simply distorted. New experiences have to be tailored to fit the existing interior world model. If we seek to relate everything new to our existing preconceptions, we constantly narrow all life experiences. If we fail to see the vividness of life and try to pigeonhole it, we ourselves become pigeonholed and trapped. If, however we are able to be open, we grow. If we attempt to relate through openness, we see things as they are in themselves and not as figments of our preconditioned framework. We can create opportunities in which inner change can take place. Our self-protective mechanisms are so subtle, we do not see them at work until we make a concerted effort to watch for them.

Meditation enables us to develop a watching consciousness; it enables us to give birth to the watcher within. Buddhism names six root delusions and 20 secondary delusions. Looking at these takes us straight back to ourselves, for there is no other place to be. The path to the Western Mysteries is traditionally opened with the injunction, 'Know Thyself'. When you are ready to seek yourself, you are ready to begin meditation in earnest. But do not be mistaken – though your quest will undoubtedly take an outer form, the journey really takes place within. Perhaps it is time for a new injunction; the path may be opened in a thousand different ways. The phrase 'I am that I am' might serve as a new starting point for, in truth, you do not have to journey to find yourself, you merely have to open your eyes to who you, as you, are. This new injunction does not prevent change or growth, it merely affirms that you can own all that you are in each and every moment. Try meditating with the phrase and see if it brings you meaning.

The six root delusions

1 Attachment: our attachment to objects exaggerates and distorts. Things seem desirable and we will spend much effort and energy in order to own or gain the object of our desires. This mental factor is difficult to eliminate.

2 Anger: anger destroys peace of mind and is harmful to the body. However, it is easier to subdue as we cannot fail to be aware of it in our lives.

3 Pride: through pride we exaggerate our own status. We want to feel special and important in some way. We believe we are

superior to others. Prideful people find it very difficult to seek help from anyone. Pride is a great obstacle to the development of the mind as it brings an attitude of mental closure.

4 Ignorance: this is considered to be the root of all delusions. It is likened to the root of a poisonous tree that produces only rotten fruit. Ignorance can only be overcome through personal effort and conscious work.

5 Negative doubt: this refers to aspects of the negative results of doubting the validity of Buddhist teaching. It is likened to someone who sets out with the intention of building a machine but soon doubts its value and ceases to work on the project rather than complete the task.

6 Mistaken views: this refers to the way in which the philosophical views we take direct behaviour and action. Mistaken views result in extreme or harmful acts, such as mortification of the body.

The root delusions named by Buddhism are the nitty-gritty of the world in which we live and move and have our being. The first four of these root delusions are the common human experiences. Who has not experienced one if not all of them at one time or another? Who has not encountered spite, jealousy and avarice? Who has not felt lack of confidence or been inattentive? The 20 secondary delusions present a long list of human frailties well known to us all. They are belligerence, vengefulness, concealment, spite, jealousy, avarice, pretence, dissimulation, self-satisfaction, cruelty, shamelessness, lack of regard for others, mental dullness, excitement, lack of confidence, laziness, unconscientiousness, forgetfulness, inattentiveness and distraction. The central questions are simple. Do we wish to continue to experience pretence, self-satisfaction and forgetfulness in ourselves? Do we wish to change aspects of ourselves? Are we willing to experience change? Are we open to the possibility of change? Do we have the commitment to implement change? These are the central questions of the integrated life, which is the ordinary life lived through the light of self-awareness.

Becoming aware of how these powerful forces work within us on a daily basis by attention and awareness constitutes the meditation of daily life. It is the great work of uniting heaven and earth. When we see things as they are, simply and unadorned by our own mental projections, we begin to admit light into the dark places. Geshe Rabten reminds us that we begin the work of self-awareness in daily life. We commence where we are at this moment in time. We do not need to plan complicated life changes or make a dramatic break with the life we already have:

> To cut oneself off from one's normal activities is not necessary. It is within the context of our everyday life that changes take place. Our ordinary life is the foundation upon which we change our mental attitude. We observe our erroneous attitude and transform it into one which is correct.[4]

EXERCISE 3.2 LOOKING WITHIN

Choose one of the root delusions as subjects for daily meditation. Try to see how this quality functions in your life. Become aware of the feelings and circumstances associated with it. Are you going to loosen the grip of this quality in your life? Stay with your chosen subject until you feel you have gained in understanding. You can always return to the same subject at a later date. When you are ready, choose another subject and examine it in the same way.

Mindful living

Mindfulness is the miracle by which we master and restore ourselves.

Thich Nhat Hanh, *The Miracle of Mindfulness*

'Mindless vandalism' is a phrase that we all recognize and understand. It means to act without thinking, to destroy for no reason, to function unconsciously. The phrase 'mindless living' may not be the stock-in-trade of the press but we can apply it all the same. What is mindless living and how can we avoid it?

Buddhism sets great store on the development of mindfulness. It is the complete opposite of mindless living. It offers specific practices. Mindfulness covers several areas: mindfulness of breathing, mindfulness of the body, mindfulness of mental content, and states of both mind and feelings. Don't let these lengthy titles mislead. These practices are neither obscure nor esoteric; they apply perfectly to the situations of everyday life. The Vietnamese monk and writer Thich Nhat Hanh understands the needs of ordinary life. He knows the pressures of everyday life:

One must prepare projects, consult with the neighbours, try to resolve a million difficulties, there is hard work to do. You might well ask: how then are we to practise mindfulness. My answer is keep your attention focused on the work, be alert and ready to handle ably and intelligently any situation which may arise – this is mindfulness.[5]

Here is the union of practice and ordinary life. Here is the integrated life in the making.

Mindfulness of breath is central to mindfulness in life, just as the breath is central to life itself. The breath can be employed in many ways. Become aware of your breath and make it your friend. Try lying down flat without a pillow, place one hand on your stomach and one hand on your upper chest. Breathe deeply and slowly until you are aware of the relationship between stomach, lungs and diaphragm. Next you can measure the length of your own breath by counting in your mind. You can then extend the length of the inhalation or exhalation. All these simple exercises develop your concentration and awareness.

Following or extending the breath really teaches you how to follow your own thoughts and extend your awareness. You can also become mindful of breathing by concentrating your attention on the physical sensation of the touch of the air that might be felt just above the upper lip or perhaps at the tip of the nose, where there is also a tiny physical movement. Such sensations are normally imperceptible. Bringing them into awareness serves to increase our sensitivity.

The same principle of paying close attention is also applied to other aspects of daily life. When developing mindfulness of feeling, we watch our reactions and responses to external stimulus on a moment-to-moment basis. Accordingly, we note how things make us feel, whether pleasant, unpleasant or indifferent. When developing mindfulness of bodily posture, we pay close attention to our own movement on a moment-to-moment basis. Quite incidentally this form of mindfulness can indirectly improve health. Posture is the basis of the Alexander Technique, which draws heavily on self-awareness of body movement. Normally we have little more than a fleeting awareness of how we sit, stand, move and walk. Check yourself now – how are you sitting? What else can you learn about your posture at this moment in time? Developing mindfulness of our mental states brings us into the area of self-observation. By watching and registering the changing states of mind we come to see ourselves. We are asked to witness our anger, guilt, fear, generosity, kindness and joy. The content of the mind is watched too in order to observe the nature of the thoughts arising. All states are observed, as a detached witness without judgement or criticism.

The phrase 'Know Thyself' takes on a new meaning in the light of mindfulness practice. How mindful are you? How mindfully do you live?

Daily awareness

The objective is to be in awareness, you must simply be aware of what you do when you are doing it, not afterwards.

Shaykh Fadhalla Heari, *The Sufi Way to Self Unfoldment*

Meditation begins in a small way as a practice of perhaps five to ten minutes. Eventually it merges with every aspect of daily life so that you develop a daily awareness of everything in your life.

Practice becomes life and life becomes practice. Awareness can be thought of as whatever you notice on a moment-to-moment basis. Living without awareness is to sleepwalk through your daily routine, but living in awareness is to be awake in life. Direct awareness is simply seeing things as they are. This is quite different from drawing upon book learning, acquired knowledge, possible theories, plausible explanations or any other intellectual constructions. Direct awareness is just about looking and seeing without embellishment. 'While sitting, I make almost no use of my intellect', writes Thich Nhat Hanh. It seems very curious that we have to practise continuously in order to develop what should be most natural to us, that is, perceiving the world about us.

Look around you now. What do you see? You will see what is in your immediate environment. The scene is probably unsurprising because you have seen it countless times before. In fact it is deeply familiar to you because you have names and concepts for everything you see. Your conceptual and linguistic understanding stands between you and the direct awareness of what is really around you. Direct awareness asks you to look without naming and to see without conceptualizing. In other words, approach everything around you as if you were seeing it for the first time. Arthur Deikman, a psychotherapist with an interest in mysticism, carried out research that shows us the difference a changed perception can make. The subjects were asked to focus their attention upon a blue vase. Not surprisingly, the vase became more vivid to the subjects. The act of just looking simply served to loosen the hold of both perception and cognition. Just being aware, even briefly, loosened the grip of the pre-existing frame of reference for 'blue' and 'vase'. This was not just any blue vase, but a particular blue vase standing in a particular spot in relation to its background, foreground and the particular qualities of light and shade in the room at a particular moment in time.[6]

This is direct awareness; it is just looking and seeing without the interference of names, labels, categories and concepts. This opens the mind to every moment and to every experience in the day. Ordinary life is about people, places, circumstances, situations and opportunities from the most mundane to the most extraordinary. See them all with awareness.

EXERCISE 3.3 BEING AWARE

Try this for yourself now as you sit. Select something in your immediate surroundings. Now just look at it as if you have never seen it before. Simply look, that's all. The intellectual mind will doubtless begin to intervene as the language of categories, comparisons and concepts comes into your mind. However, just look and just see.

If you saw something new in your chosen object, then you were open to the possibility of finding something new. New awareness can only arise where there is space in the mind. New awareness can only break through when you are perfectly focused in the moment as it is happening. Just pay attention to the moment. How soon is it before the moment has passed?

> Don't chase after the past,
> Don't seek the future;
> The past is gone,
> The future hasn't come.
> But see clearly on the spot
> The object which is now,
> While finding and living in
> A still, unmoving state of mind.
>   The Buddha

Paying attention means just seeing things as they are without embellishment or overlay. This breaks down our categorizing habits. Each object is merely itself. Moreover, giving attention to the unfolding moments of daily life serves as a brake on our wilder passions, flights of fancy and rash decisions that arise in the heat of the moment and then deflate like burst balloons in the cold light of day. Paying attention to the moment frees us from both the past and the future. How much time is wasted daily as we relive past encounters and anticipate future outcomes? Live in the moment with awareness. Set about establishing the integrated life for yourself.

04

developing: the greater blueprint

> The cosmos is a pattern. So are we.
>
> William Gray, *The Ladder of Lights*

Patterns for living

It is easy to become bogged down in the nitty-gritty of life. Quite simply we become so closely focused upon our own lives that we cannot look up to gain an overview of life itself. We see the parts but not the whole. In other words, we fail to see the wood for the trees, as the proverb says. Yet even a moment's reflection reveals the great impersonal currents that are common to all human life regardless of time or place. Birth and death are the twin poles of our existence. Birth is a wonderful mystery. Death is seen as a terrible mystery. Between these two points, humanity knows joy and suffering, fear and surrender, love and hate, loss and gain. Universal patterns repeat time and time again.

The drive to make sense of our place in the world seems to be a deeply rooted impulse. We do not live in isolation but through a network of complex biological, emotional, social and spiritual relationships. Our capacity to forge relationships extends into the world. Key moments in the passing of time such as the New Year or the equinox and solstice markers have been important shared celebrations. We feel an instinctive drive to relate to transpersonal markers in order to understand our own place in the greater scheme. Denying these greater transpersonal markers in order to build a purely utilitarian social order serves to repress these instincts, which reappear with great force as soon as social control weakens. Contemplating a bigger picture puts a different perspective on the personal life as we realize that our dilemmas and struggles are universal. Touching an overview lifts our eyes from the immediate to the long term and we can contemplate life as something more than a day-to-day experience.

Attempts to portray our complex interrelationship to one another, to the world and to the divine are varied, ancient and universal. Myths and magic, ceremony and observance, festival and offering are all attempts at relating to the transpersonal and the invisible. Such acts recognize a place in the wider scheme. To acknowledge this is to accept that a relationship is possible and potentially meaningful. Theistic traditions equate God with the bigger picture; non-theistic traditions equate an Absolute Reality with the bigger picture. We should not expect to find the complexity of the cosmic expressed through the cut and dried language of simple reason. To contemplate the vast themes of infinite time, endless space and human nature is to acknowledge wonder, mystery, awe and paradox. We are no longer in the realm of the literal where sufficient information serves our needs, but we have moved into symbolic, poetic and metaphorical language. This alone can express the inexpressible. The human imagination has created many such models, which have been depicted in many forms from the diagrammatic to the architectural, from the secret to the open, from the literary to the oral. Some have stood the test of time and proved to be sturdy maps for other travellers who have sought the same journey.

The Wheel of Becoming: a monastic way

What O Monks, is the origin of suffering? It is that craving which rise to ever fresh rebirth.

Digha-Nikaya XXII

The Tibetan Wheel of Life, which is more properly called the Wheel of Becoming, expresses the central beliefs of Buddhism in visual form. It is to be found painted on the vestibule wall of all Tibetan monasteries. This image is a cosmogram, which relates the individual to the whole. It is a picture of cause and effect. Consciousness is the key that determines all outcomes. The Wheel is divided into four concentric circles. The hub depicts the root forces that bind the individual to the wheel. The next circle shows the effects of mind upon material outcome. The third wheel depicts six planes of consciousness. Finally, the fourth and outer circle shows the 12 links that create karma and result in bondage to the wheel. The wheel itself is a powerful symbol of endless cycle and motion. It turns relentlessly time after time. This is **samsara**, the cycle of being, incarnation after incarnation. Liberation comes with release from the wheel.

In the centre at the hub of the wheel, three animals endlessly chase each other. The cockerel, snake and pig are trapped together, forever biting each other's tail. The red cockerel symbolizes greed and lust. The green snake symbolizes anger and hatred. The black pig symbolizes ignorance and delusion. These images represent the three qualities which, according to Buddhism, keep the individual pinned to the wheel. Greed and lust are never satisfied. Hatred knows no bounds. Ignorance keeps us blind. Sometimes the snake and cockerel are shown

figure 4.1 the Wheel of Life

emerging together from the mouth of the pig, indicating that
ignorance and delusion give birth to greed and hatred. Around
this inner circle is another circle, which is half-black and half-
white. In the white half people ascend and in the black half they
fall. These symbolize positive and negative karma, which lead to
fortunate and unfortunate rebirths. The next wheel is divided
into six segments depicting planes of consciousness, the world
of gods, titans, hungry ghosts, the hells, the animal kingdom
and the world of humans. Finally, the last and outer wheel

shows 12 causes, which give rise to karmic factors. These are called The Twelve Links of Interdependent Origination.

In the first picture, ignorance is represented by a blind man. The second picture shows a potter symbolizing the making of karmic formations. The third picture shows a monkey jumping wildly to represent the untrained consciousness. The fourth picture shows a person drinking alcohol to symbolize attachment. The fifth picture depicts a monkey picking fruit from a tree to represent constant grasping. The sixth picture shows a woman about to give birth. She represents the principle of becoming. The karmic forces that have been carried are now ready to take their place and come to birth. The seventh picture depicts consciousness as it leaves the after-death state, the **bardo**, to enter incarnation at birth. The eighth picture shows a boat, which represents name and form, the form that carries consciousness from life to life. The ninth picture shows a building as yet uninhabited, symbolizing the six senses, the sense organs awaiting consciousness. The tenth picture shows a man and woman in physical embrace. The eleventh drawing depicts a person shot in the eye with an arrow to show the painful reality of gross sensation. The final image, not surprisingly, depicts old age and death.

The wheel is clutched by Yama, the Lord of Death, who represents primal delusion. We are in his grip until we make a conscious choice to become free from the cycle of life and death. Outside the wheel to the right stands the figure of the Buddha, who has attained liberation. He points to the moon, which symbolizes the cool light of enlightenment or sometimes to another wheel of eight spokes, which is the wheel of **dharma**. Both images are placed to the left of the Wheel of Life.

Although the Wheel of Becoming is a presentation of Buddhist teaching, we too can benefit from this model. Its central theme is that of cause and effect in human consciousness. So take this as your theme for meditation. It can be approached in many ways. You can find your own way, as meditation does not always need to be prescriptive. Begin to contemplate how the subtle forces of cause and effect are at work in your life. The wheel is a universal symbol that lends itself to a visual meditation. It reminds you that everything turns.

The Tree of Life: a mystical way

> The Tree of Life, as cannot be too often emphasized, is
> not so much a system as a method.
>
> Dion Fortune, *The Mystical Qabalah*

As the Wheel of Life serves as a cosmogram, which is a symbolic
depiction of both individual and cosmic forces, so the Tree of
Life also serves in the same way. Unlike Buddhism, which has a
very clear beginning through the life of Prince Siddhartha
Gautama, the Buddha, the origins of *Qabalah*, or *Kabbalah*, are
to be found in early metaphysical speculations and practices.
Kabbalah developed as an oral tradition. Its key text, the *Sepher
Yetzirah* did not appear in printed form until 1558. Indeed the
very name, *Kabbalah*, which is derived from *Qbl*, refers to the
oral nature of the tradition and means 'to receive'. In complete
contrast to Buddhism, *Kabbalah* has always been a hidden
current. It evolved as a persecuted philosophy carried by a
persecuted people. A written tradition meant danger, but a
concealed tradition brought safety. A complete metaphysical
doctrine and philosophy is presented in symbolic form. This is
the Tree of Life, the *Otz Chiim*.

We commonly speak of the spiritual journey. The Tree of Life
can be likened to a roadmap for the path ahead. It is a map of
both the individual and the whole. As mundane maps show
roads and conurbations, the Tree of Life depicts Paths and
Sephiroth. The Sephiroth, the Divine Emanations, represent the
outpouring of creation from the unmanifest towards the
manifestation. The 10 Sephiroth, the 10 aspects of being, are
connected through 22 Paths. This is the Tree of Life and this is
the spiritual journey.

Together, the Sephiroth and the Paths form the map of being. As
streets and towns have names and occupants, so the Paths and
Sephiroth also have names and qualities that express particular
aspects of being, which are simultaneously both individual and
transpersonal. The Tree is travelled much like an internal map,
its inner landscape being internalized through meditation. Its
many symbols are integrated into the psyche. As we integrate its
experiences, we unfold these same characteristics within
ourselves. The Tree of Life is therefore a personal journey of
discovery. It is truly the Great Adventure. The World Tree is
another universal symbol that lends itself to visual meditation.

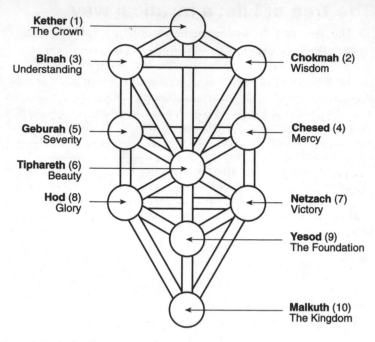

figure 4.2 the Sephiroth upon the Tree of Life

The Tree of Life map is unfolded through many meditations upon the symbols attributed to both the Sephiroth and Paths. Dion Fortune expresses this relationship succinctly for us:

EXERCISE 4.1 THE TREE OF LIFE

Sit quietly and enter meditation. Use the following words, which are taken from the **Zohar**, to create your own imagery:

In the beginning, the House of the World was made. This House forms the centre of the universe, and it has many doors and entrance chambers on all sides, sacred and exalted abodes where the celestial birds build their nests, each according to its kind.

From the midst of the House rises a large tree, with mighty branches and an abundance of fruit providing fruit for all, which rears itself to the clouds of heaven and is lost to view between three rocks from which the tree again emerges, so

---

that it is both above and below them. From this Tree the House is watered.

In this House are stored many precious and undiscovered treasures. That Tree is visible in the daytime, but hidden at night.

When you have created your own image of the House of the World and the Tree of Life, begin to contemplate what you see in the mind's eye. Let the House of the World and Tree of Life radiate a powerful vitality. As you watch, the Tree of Life seems to grow from its foundation within the House of the World. Its branches extend towards you, its leaves unfurl. Lush fruits ripen before your gaze. Their perfume fills the air. You reach up and pick a fruit, it comes away from the Tree with ease. You eat the fruit and savour its flavour. Its nourishment fills your being with sweet delight and vitality.

Each symbol upon the Tree represents a cosmic force or factor, when the mind concentrates upon it, it comes into touch with that force, in other words a surface channel, a channel in consciousness has been made between the conscious mind of the individual and a particular factor in the world-soul.[1]

It is clear that a long process of meditation is required in order to integrate the Tree as an internal model. This demands a level of commitment and genuine spiritual aspiration. Like Buddhism, Kabbalah is a living tradition. If it calls to you it is possible to find teachers and guides. Even at the simplest level the Tree of Life offers us many subjects for meditation:

1 *Kether*/The Crown: take the source of all life as your theme
2 *Chokmah*/Wisdom: take wisdom as your theme
3 *Binah*/Understanding: take universal understanding as your theme
4 *Chesed*/Mercy: take mercy as your theme
5 *Geburah*/Severity: take severity as your theme
6 *Tiphareth*/Beauty: take mystical consciousness as your theme
7 *Netzach*/Victory: take emotional and instinctive drives as your theme
8 *Hod*/Glory: take the reasoning mind as your theme
9 *Yesod*/The Foundation: take the subconscious mind as your theme

10 *Malkuth*/The Kingdom: take physical manifestation as your theme

These ten introductory themes are no more than a brief glimpse into the world of *Kabbalah*. *Kabbalah* offers the opportunity for a lifetime's study through the unfolding of the self. It is truly the Tree of Life. Its fruits await your picking.

Unfolding the lotus: an esoteric way

> The man of perfection is one who can move through all these seven chakras easily.
>
> Osho, *The Heart Sutra*

The word **chakra** has been appearing steadily over the past decade. Despite being a Sanskrit word it has now become a familiar term in the contemporary vocabulary of modern Western spirituality. Such easy familiarity should not blind us to the fact that this particular esoteric map was kept secret for a long time. The work of unfolding this particular blueprint was considered so delicate that it could only be undertaken through the special relationship between teacher and pupil. There is some sense in this view. Spiritual blueprints serve to create change in every aspect of daily living. Internalizing any spiritual blueprint is achieved through the interior processes of meditation and contemplation. As we integrate the model within ourselves, we are changed in the process. We have to be willing and able to accept the changes this brings.

The word 'chakra' simply means 'wheel'. The chakra is also described as a lotus, or **padma**. The lotus as a symbol shares much in common with the rose; its many petals represent the flowering of the human being. Unlike the rose, however, the lotus is rooted in the underwater mud and reaches for the light as it grows. Finally, it flowers upon the surface. The pattern symbolizes well the journey of the human soul. We too are rooted in the earth and aspire to the light. A full knowledge of the chakras forms a complete branch of metaphysics. However, even the novice can gain something from this particular blueprint. All blueprints require a certain intellectual grasp at first. When the overall structure has been understood the map is handed over to the interior senses through meditation. So let us first gain a brief intellectual overview of the subject.

The physical form is interpenetrated by subtle non-physical energies. The main chakras can be thought of as locations where

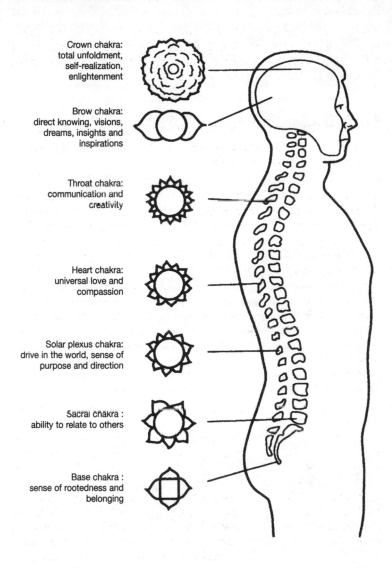

Crown chakra:
total unfoldment,
self-realization,
enlightenment

Brow chakra:
direct knowing, visions,
dreams, insights and
inspirations

Throat chakra:
communication and
creativity

Heart chakra:
universal love and
compassion

Solar plexus chakra:
drive in the world, sense of
purpose and direction

Sacral chakra :
ability to relate to others

Base chakra :
sense of rootedness and
belonging

figure 4.3 the chakras

these subtle energies are especially concentrated and active. Bearing this in mind, we find chakras located at the base of the spine, at the reproductive centre, at the solar plexus, the heart, the throat and the brow. The seventh centre is located at the crown of the head in the space slightly above the actual head. This centre is often distinguished from the other six and treated as the unique centre of consciousness. As the subtle energies interpenetrate the physical body, each centre is concerned with a wide number of activities that range from physical function to a spiritual quality.

As we unfold this particular blueprint within ourselves, the qualities and functions of each of the centres begins to operate more fully in our lives and consciousness. It is possible to use the qualities and functions of each chakra as themes for a series of meditations. As we draw upon this model we unfold the lotus of our own being. Use each meditation separately.

EXERCISE 4.2 THE SEVEN LIGHTS

1 The *Muladhara* chakra

Sit comfortably and become aware of the area at the base of the spine. When you are settled begin to contemplate your relationship to the physical world around you. What does this level of existence mean to you? Allow images of the physical earth to arise in your mind. *Muladhara* means 'root'. Contemplation on this centre involves a quiet awareness of our sense of rootedness into the earth. Simply close your meditation when you have contemplated your relationship to the earth.

2 The *Svadisthana* chakra

This time focus your inner awareness just above the base of the spine. Settle into your own meditation and begin to contemplate the way in which you are able to relate to others. Do you find this easy or difficult? Do you sustain relationships over a long period? Do you give yourself in a relationship? This chakra is related to all the close relationships that we create. *Svadisthana* means 'sweetness' or 'one's own abode'. Both titles reflect the intimate function of this chakra. Violation at this level of being is indeed a total violation of 'one's own abode'.

3 The *Manipura* chakra

To meditate on this chakra place your awareness deep in the abdomen. This area is often known as the solar plexus. Enter your own meditative state and contemplate how you exercise your own true will in life. Are you wilful or do you use will in harmony with your sense of the divine will. The Sanskrit name of this centre, *manipura*, means 'lustrous gem' or 'city of jewels'. The solar plexus chakra is a storehouse of subtle energy. This centre should glow and radiate like a shining gem or bowl of jewels piled high.

4 The *Anahata* chakra

To meditate on this chakra become aware of the heart centre. This is the centre of transpersonal and unconditional love. When you meditate on this centre take unconditional love as your focus. Ask yourself where is your unconditional love? This is not the personal love of a relationship, but the extension of deep and generous loving kindness to others. *Anahata* means 'unstruck'. It refers to a sound that is heard but not struck, a subtle reference to the more sensitized qualities of this chakra. Only a sensitized ear hears a delicate note.

5 The *Vishuddi* chakra

Sit quietly in meditation and become aware of the area of the throat. This is clearly connected to the function of speech, which in turn is related to the kinds of thought which arise within you. Reflect upon how you communicate. What do you talk about? How do you express yourself? Do you always say what you mean and mean what you say? *Vishuddi* means 'to purify'. This principle can be applied to the power of speech and communication to distinguish between those words and thoughts that are allied to a purpose and those that are no more than meaningless noises.

6 The *Ajna* chakra

Sit quietly in meditation and become aware of the brow centre. This is traditionally the place of the third eye. *Ajna* means 'to know'. This refers to the ability to know things accurately and directly without deductive or discursive thought. Contemplate the significance of higher states of consciousness for the evolution of humanity.

7 The *Sahasrara* chakra

This chakra is often treated quite separately from the first six. When you meditate upon it think of the space slightly above the head. *Sahasrara* means 'thousandfold'. This chakra is shown as an open lotus with a thousand petals to symbolize the idea that a human being has an unlimited number of qualities to unfold. In your meditation contemplate the idea of potential and fulfilment. The *Sahasrara* chakra is like the spiritual crown, the crowning achievement of your being.

These basic meditations are designed merely to put you in touch with the basic principle of each chakra. Once you have integrated a basic understanding, it becomes possible to move on to a more complex interaction. Traditionally, each of the chakras is represented through a number of interrelated symbols. The functions and nature of each centre are described not through words but through symbolic images. These symbols need to be internalized through meditation. Animal and elemental symbols are attributed to the first five chakras. These express something of the nature and quality of the chakra. A sounded meditation, a **mantra**, is also attributed to six of the seven centres. Sounding or vibrating the mantra has the power to awaken the chakra more deeply than a merely intellectual approach. Additionally, further symbolism continues to describe and enshrine the qualities and powers of each of the centres. As the symbols become deeply internalized through meditation the centres are opened a little further.

These meditations have the power to open a door into a new world. If you find that this sevenfold blueprint calls to you, take the opportunity to read, study and meditate. Be thankful that this blueprint is no longer the hidden secret of former times. It is accessible.

The Natural Blueprint

As Above so Below.

Hermetic axiom

The Hermetic axiom, 'As Above so Below', admits us to an open secret, that the universe partakes of a holographic nature. This deceptively simple phrase links the individual with the whole, the lesser with the greater, the microcosm with the macrocosm. It serves at once to establish a fundamental connection that has proved itself to be the springboard for much human inspiration and creativity. The uniting of the above and the below bridges the sense of separation that now haunts us in so many ways.

If every part reflects the whole to which it belongs, then the greater may be seen in the lesser. We see this simply demonstrated in the body which holds maps of the whole in its parts: reflexology is based on the foot as a map of the whole; palmistry is based on the palm of the hand as a map of the whole; iridology is based upon the iris of the eye as a map of the whole. Other maps surely await discovery.

The human body as microcosm is an ancient and universal theme. The Sanksrit text, the *Siva Samhita*, describes the body as a symbolic landscape. In Chapter 11, (verses 1–4), we find that the body takes on a cosmic nature:

> In this body, the mount Meru, i.e. the vertebral column, is surrounded by seven islands; there are rivers, seas, mountains, fields; and lords of the fields too.

> There are in it seers and sages; all the stars and planets as well. There are sacred pilgrimages, shrines; and presiding deities of the shrines.

> The sun and moon, agents of creation and destruction, also move in it. Ether, air, fire, water and earth are also there.

> All the beings that exist in the three worlds are also to be found in the body; surrounding the Meru, they are engaged in their respective functions.

Through analogy the whole body has been seen as a symbolic mirror of a greater reality. The relationship between the parts and the whole again expresses the eternal relationship between unity and division, between the one and the many. The interdependence within the body reflects the interdependence of nature herself. The proportions of the human body have long been of interest to the spiritually awakened. The Egyptians and artists of the Renaissance used a canon of 18, dividing the body from feet to brow into nine squares. This strict mathematical code was imbedded in the beautiful and the sacred. Proportion was rendered into three dimensional geometry: relationships between arm span, upper body and total height provided key measures. The placement of the navel in the body provided another significant mathematical relationship as ratio became pattern.

This natural blueprint has been repeatedly unfolded in sacred art and architecture of diverse and unrelated civilizations. As a sacred place, the temple has been constructed to exemplify the body of the spirit, the outer container for the ineffable. The analogy is self-evident, the human body and the body of the temple express the one life through the universal language of sacred measure. The expression, 'the body is the temple of the spirit', is frequently repeated but probably most often misunderstood. It almost implies that the body is hollow and awaits filling, but body and spirit are already united and cannot be separated. The divine marriage of spirit and substance has

EXERCISE 4.3 THE HUMAN MANDALA

figure 4.4 you are a star

Using the human body as a mandala, a sacred pattern, is to resacralize form and restore meaning to everything the body can do. Imagine yourself standing with arms and legs outstretched. See how your body forms a five-pointed star. You are a star. Begin your meditation by contemplating the feet and their daily work of putting you in touch with the earth. How often do you walk upon the earth? How well do you look after your feet? Contemplate the legs that carry you in life. Are they strong and confident? Move your awareness into your trunk. Contemplate the work of your own excretion system. This part of you is most likely to be taken for granted. Move your awareness into your feelings to relate here. Contemplate your physical sexual nature. How have you used this power? A woman can contemplate the womb and the monthly cycle, which sustains the life-giving process. Continue moving through the body, moving your awareness into as many parts of the body as you wish. There is plenty to meditate on and you will not tire of subjects when using the human form as your mandala. Contemplate organs in relation to one another and in relation to the whole. Contemplate functions and abilities. Choose your own subjects. There is much to discover.

already taken place in every cell. 'The body is the most dense expression of mind, and mind is all the subtle extensions of body; and underlying this entire world, from the most dense to the most subtle there is one substance.'[2] Christian churches, Hindu temples and Buddhist stupas all embody sacred proportion expressed through architectural form. The Hindu architectural sutra says, 'The Universe is present in the temple by means of proportion.' The human body is itself a sacred blueprint, rich with meaning and significance. Its measure is sacred measure. It is only secular architecture that corresponds to the utilitarian and mundane.

The secular world has lost sight of the natural blueprint, the human form itself. The natural blueprint is neither hidden nor distant; it has become veiled from us as our collective sight has looked away towards other distractions and amusements. Perhaps as we continue to experience our own twenty-first century renaissance, our sight will once more become refocused on the sacred nature of our own being as blueprint of the cosmos. The Anthropos, like a constant heartbeat, has historically inspired varied and diverse forms of creation through music, art, dance, song, sacred iconography and sacred building. Perhaps it will do so again.

These blueprints, which at first seem so different, have much in common. Each unites the individual with the greater whole. Each represents a path of unification. Each offers a spiritual path that has already been walked by the disciples and sages, aspirants and devotees of previous generations. Each points you towards a bigger picture.

05
deepening: the way of the heart

The more the heart is an avid void, the more abundantly light will shine into it.

Thich Nhat Hanh, *The Sun My Heart*

The knowing heart

Who do you care for? Who do you love? Who loves you? You know the answer to these questions with a certainty that needs nothing more. The heart knows, it is as simple as that. It is not surprising that many cultures have identified the seat of the soul with the heart. In these times we seem to have lost contact with the knowing of the heart and the seat of the soul. We are mystified by the mystical and shy at talk of the soul. Instead, we value the cold rationalization of the intellect. We fear the knowing of the heart. It defies logic. The spiritual traditions of the world have each kept the flame of the heart alive in their own way. Even when the practice falls short of the ideal, the ideal remains. Christianity is perceived as an outflowing of love to the world. Buddhism is based on the generation of compassion. The heart takes us beyond the confines of the self towards a universal realization of connectivity. It takes us beyond rationality, which knows nothing of love.

We may gain insight into the spiritual heart by looking at the ideas related to the heart chakra. The heart centre, the *Anahata* chakra is symbolized by the element of air. It is represented by the gazelle, the animal which leaps through the air. We cannot survive without air, yet it cannot be seen. Its invisibility does not make it any less real. We perceive the air through its effects. We are immersed in air and partake of a dynamic exchange continuously. The air around us cannot be owned, it is shared by all. Here we have a symbol of universal love and compassion in the world. Love is known only through its effects, but is itself invisible. The *Anahata* chakra has some particular characteristics which are significant. It contains a psychic knot known as the **Vishnu Granthi**. This indicates that the active powers of the heart chakra are not awakened, except through the expansion of consciousness. This alone has the power to dissolve the knot. Buddhism recognizes this fact and presents lengthy training in the generation of compassion. Whereas we might accept varying degrees of compassion as another mark of difference between people, Buddhism shows that compassion can be born in us all through successive changes in consciousness. Personal love is readily explained and readily experienced, but transpersonal love is rare. It has no personal investment, it seeks no reward, it requires nothing, it demands nothing in return. Yet we instinctively recognize it when we see it in the lives of the truly great. Personal love takes us towards this greater understanding, but a yawning gulf remains between these different manifestations. The tradition of *Kabbalah* also recognizes how difficult it is to open the heart. To awaken the heart we must cross an abyss in ourselves that is represented on the Tree of Life as the Veil of Paroketh. In other words, we cannot cross to the heart without making a great transition from the individual to the universal. It is immensely difficult to make this leap from personal to transpersonal and universal love. For most of us the powers of the heart remain largely dormant.

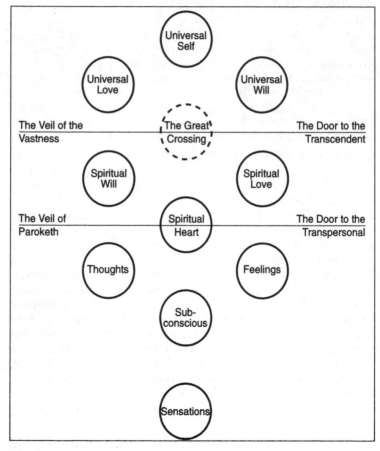

figure 5.1 the spiritual body

Unlike all other chakras, the *Anahata* chakra is represented with a subsidiary centre, which is described as a red lotus with eight petals. It is symbolized by an island of gems with an altar set beneath a great tree, the *kalpa* tree, which is the wish-fulfilling tree. It is here that devotion is offered in meditation to the guru or spiritual teacher. This minor centre represents the opening quality that only devotion offered outside the self can bring. It is said that when the powers of the *Anahata* chakra are active, all wishes may be granted. However, this centre may only become active once there are no more desires for the self. As the Tibetan says, 'Seek nothing for the separated self.' The transition of identity from the small self to the greater whole is a central concern of all spiritual traditions. Each tradition accomplishes this transition according to its own light. Christianity offers Christ as the model of universal love who sought nothing for the separated self. Buddhism offers a long process of transition through meditation. Much change is effected where the teacher–pupil relationship functions.

Opening the heart

That man who attains to the secret of unity
who is not detained at the stages on the road.
your being is naught but thorns and weeds,
cast it all away from you
go sweep out the chamber of your heart,
make it ready to be the dwelling place of the beloved
when you depart out, he will enter in
in you, void of yourself will he display his beauty.
Mahmud Shabastri, *The Secret Garden*

The opening of the heart is rarely accompanied without personal suffering and pain. The rose with its thorns universally symbolizes the trials and pains of love both personal and mystical. As the lotus exemplifies the spiritual traditions of the East, so the rose has become the central hallmark of Western spirituality. It is identified with the Virgin Mary as she is called the Rose of Heaven. The Rose of Sharon is the Church itself. Curiously, roses were also sacred to Isis. In the classical novel, *The Golden Ass*, the central character Lucius is finally restored from the bestial state into which he has fallen through eating from a garland of roses.

The rose has a long history in the Western tradition. The Rosicrucian movement combined the rose and the cross into a

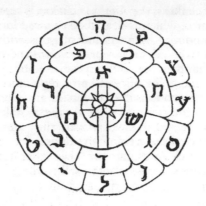

figure 5.2 the Rose of the West

profound symbol of divine love flowering upon the cross of the
world. The Golden Dawn, a later historical manifestation of the
same spiritual impetus, again took the rosy-cross as a central
symbol, the rose blooming upon a golden cross. The five petals
of the rose represent the four elements of earth, air, fire and
water, activated and ruled by the fifth element of spirit. The rose
is drawn with a total of 22 letters arranged in three rows of
three, seven and 12 letters, which make up the full letters of the
Hebrew alphabet. The mystic rose stands for the entire universe.
Like the thousand-petalled lotus, the rose represents
completion, fulfilment and the bloom of the spiritual within the
material.

EXERCISE 5.1 THE ROSE OF THE HEART

The opening of the rose makes a wonderful subject for a meditation.

Sit in meditation and become aware of your heart centre. In your
mind's eye place a rosebud at the heart centre. As you watch, see
the rosebud gently unfurl its petals. Let each petal represent a
quality of loving. When the rose of the heart is founded and fully
open allow yourself to generate feelings of universal love. Radiate
this subtle quality like rose perfume. Let it be carried on the air.
Let the rose bloom in the heart.

As the exercise shows, compassion grows from the chamber of
the heart. The Sanskrit word for compassion is *karuna*, which
is derived from the root *kr*, which implies action. Indeed, how
can true compassion exist without the impulsion to act? Service

might be thought of as compassion in action, though this might be thought rather old fashioned in today's fast moving world. If the concept of service appears outworn, we only have to imagine ourselves living in a society in which this ideal has totally faded. Values of self-aggrandisement, selfishness, survival, power and greed instead become the norm. Those too weak, too poor or too disadvantaged cannot compete in the human jungle. Who will serve them? Some might well argue that we have already created this world. Currently, the marketplace offers no morality except that of the right price and the short term. The cult of individuality has been raised to a fine art. Service implies an awareness of others.

It is always easy to favour those whom we know and like. It is difficult to extend kindness to those who are strangers to us or those we may dislike. We have to work actively to overcome our feelings. Buddhism recognizes that cherishing others is so unusual and difficult to achieve; it can only be developed through mental training. An attitude of altruism based on love and compassion for all living things can only grow if we work to overcome those beliefs and blocks that serve as hindrances. Our education and upbringing teaches us to look after ourselves first, to compete with others and to believe in ourselves. We have to make an effort to extend our thoughts towards those who we do not know and will never meet.

Opening the heart does not come from being clever but from simplicity. It does not come from being knowledgeable but from being wise. It does not come from being full of self but from being empty of self. How difficult it is to live with an open heart in a society that values the clever, the knowledgeable and the egocentric. There are many meditations on the heart and its awakening. Although the particulars may vary from tradition to tradition the same themes are universally expressed. The heart is seen as the meeting place of the human and the divine or the universal. The chamber of the heart becomes the inner sanctuary where peace is contemplated. We find an extraordinary similarity in the advice given by Isha Schwaller de Lubicz and Thich Naht Hanh. When speaking of the ancient Egyptian tradition, Isha Schwaller de Lubicz says, 'Meditation on the spiritual heart should begin with an intense effort to identify one's own heart with the heart of the cosmos, which is our source of light and life.'[1] While Thich Naht Hanh suggests, 'Look at the immense light we call the sun, if it stops shining the flow of our life will also stop, and so the sun is our second heart, our heart outside of our body.'² Both writers look for the spiritual heart in the simple. Simplicity of heart is the open-heartedness of a child looking upon the world with new eyes. The devotion of the heart is a deep feeling of overwhelming love. The following exercise is about discovering where our devotion might be. It is possible to repeat this exercise over a period of time as consciousness changes. It is initially quite common to find nothing that calls upon the deep transpersonal devotion of the heart.

EXERCISE 5.2 FINDING DEVOTION

Sit quietly for a few moments until you feel deeply centred in yourself. Place your hand over the heart and become attuned to your own heartbeat. In your mind's eye create the following scene. Find yourself standing in a sacred location of your own choosing. This might be a quiet meadow, secluded grove, rocky peninsula, ancient temple, church, chapel, empty room or any other location. Spend some time creating this sacred place in your mind's eye and if you cannot relate to the term 'sacred' just create a quiet place where you would feel at home. Create this ideal location as fully as you can in your mind, adding any necessary details from either memory or imagination to make it come alive for you. Next, move to the centre where you will find a table covered with a cloth. Let the cloth be a colour of your own choosing and the table any dimension and type that you wish. Using your creative imagination light a single candle and place it on the table.

Now enter more deeply into your own mind. Begin to reflect on where and how you have given your love. Who do you love deeply and without limit? Doubtless the first images to come to mind will be loved ones, family and close friends. Allow yourself to see all the faces and names. Eventually this list of loved ones will be complete; imagine a group photo of all these special people and place it on the table. Continue to reflect upon your love and how and where it is given beyond the circle of loved ones and friends. What calls upon your heart now? As personal love is left behind, human causes, transpersonal issues and even global concerns may come to mind. With each realization, once again embody the idea in a symbolic photo and place it on the table. Continue asking the same question of yourself until you feel emptied. Finally, survey the table at the centre of your own sacred space. What do you find there?

Finding the seed of compassion

Without a seed there will be no plant.

Geshe Rabten, *The Treasury of Dharma*

The first move towards a more universal understanding comes as we are able to look beyond the immediate self. It is so easy to value ourselves and to always put our own needs above all else. Buddhism specifically applies a brake to this egocentric view by promoting the sentiency of all beings. This teaching asks that we value and cherish non-human forms of life from the great to the small. Such teaching has a profound and real impact in the world. It is impossible, for instance, to imagine Buddhists engaging in big game hunting. At a time of endangered species and diminishing habitats, we need a philosophy to sustain our efforts against the logic of the marketplace. Buddhism suggests that we treat all sentient beings as if they had been good mothers to us. The thought is powerful, even startling. It provides a good starting point for the development of altruism. Valuing other life encourages us to find a shared place in the greater world; we do not have to own or exploit, we merely have to learn to cooperate. As we take others into account more often, so the resulting expansion of consciousness and being opens the mind and heart. Compassion is born when the personality self gives way. Thich Naht Hanh finds a simple reverence in the most ordinary of creatures:

> Watching a green caterpillar on a leaf, we understand the importance of the caterpillar, not just from our self-centred point of view as a human but from the penetration based on the interdependence of all things. Realizing the preciousness of all life and every being. We dare not deprive the caterpillar of its life, if some day we kill a caterpillar we will feel as if we are killing ourselves that something of ourselves dies with the caterpillar.[3]

instinctively recognize the diminution that self-centredness and hard-heartedness produce. As a society we need to be able to nourish compassion in any way that we can. It is a fragile enough quality in the times in which we live. In a civilization where technology is crucial for success, there is little room for compassion. When you find the seeds of compassion in yourself then you have made a contribution to the greater whole. If you can keep this flame alive, it will inspire others. The Lucis Trust reminds us of the value of the individual: 'As each takes his or her own step forwards into a more inclusive and compassionate

understanding, he or she helps to lift the human family nearer to its spiritual destiny.'4 Too often we feel that our small contribution makes no difference. Recognizing one's own spiritual nature allows the individual to recognize divinity in others and in all forms of life. The following meditation is a modified version of a Buddhist exercise. Its purpose is to develop an awareness that assists us to exchange one's self for others.

EXERCISE 5.3 TAKING AND GIVING

Sit quietly, close your eyes and become attuned to your own heart centre. Now imagine a golden vessel at the heart. When this is established begin to visualize the mass of sentient beings gathering. The Buddhist form employs beings from the six realms depicted upon the Wheel of Becoming. The same purpose can be achieved by imagining a host of beings, both human and animal, gathering at the heart. Each being is drawn to the heart centre out of a need. As the group nestles around the grail of the heart, so these needs become expressed through the breath of the group, which is visualized as a dark vapour arising from the group. As you breathe in, the needs of the group are drawn into the heart centre. Their collected breath is drawn into your own heart centre. While holding the group need within the heart, generate love and compassion. On your own outbreath, imagine radiant light pouring through the centre to encompass the group. Continue taking and giving in this way. At the close see the sentient beings enveloped in light returning to the world and allow the grail of the heart to fade.

Geshe Rabten writes:

> This practice helps us develop both the proper attitude towards others and also the power of the mind. Perhaps someone may have doubts about its effectiveness and say it's only an imaginative process and doesn't actually benefit others directly, at all. While it's quite true that this will not benefit others directly, it does nonetheless develop the mind in a very positive way and it benefits sentient beings indirectly in a very positive way. In other words, if we have already created a strong force for compassion within ourselves, we are more willing and able to act in the real world when called upon.5

Unlimited friendliness: the *Metta Sutta*

> The extra smile, that extra kindness can mean so much to people. This is practice.
>
> Ani Tenzin Palmo, *Walking on Lotus Flowers*

When were you last kind to someone? When was someone kind to you? Kindness is a simple virtue quite without pretension or expectation. It is an act of openness, simplicity and unlimited friendliness. Yet it is clear that as individuals we are not as kind to one another as we might be, otherwise this simple virtue would require no special teaching. The development of kindness is a part of Buddhist practice. The Dalai Lama has even said, 'My religion is kindness.' Throughout the countries of Southeast Asia monks daily recite the *Metta Sutta*. Here is a simple expression of unlimited kindness and goodwill to others. The words are attributed to the Buddha himself:

> This is the Work of those who are Skilled and Peaceful who seek the good:
> May they be able and upright, straightforward, of gentle speech and not proud.
> May they be content and easily supported, unburdened with their senses calmed.
> May they be wise, not arrogant and without desire for the possessions of others.
> May they do nothing mean or that the wise would reprove.
>
> May all beings be happy.
> May they live in safety and joy.
> All living beings, whether weak or strong, tall or stout, medium or short, seen or unseen, near or distant, born to be born, may they all be happy.
>
> Let no one deceive another or despise any being in any state, let none by anger or hatred wish harm to another.
>
> As a mother watches over her child, willing to risk her own life to protect her only child, so with a boundless heart should one cherish all living beings, suffusing the whole world with unobstructed loving kindness.
>
> Standing or walking, sitting or lying down, during all one's waking hours, may one remain mindful of this heart and this way of living that is the best in the world.

Unattached to speculations, views and sense desires, with clear vision,
such a person will never be reborn in the
cycles of suffering.

It is perhaps salutary to know that today as every other day, the collective heart of Buddhist Southeast Asia wishes us all well. We in turn can choose to wish others well and also show kindness to those whom we encounter. There can be little doubt that the positive force of love is the single spiritual quality that all religions are agreed about. Indeed, who could disagree with the significance given to the power of love? We ourselves need love as children and adults, as parents and grandparents. Everyone benefits from the open loving heart. We can put this simple faith into practice through the meditation of the loving heart.

EXERCISE 5.4 RADIATING LOVE

In order to radiate love, we need first to experience the same feeling within ourselves. It often proves to be the case that as children we did not feel valued and loved. So before radiating love to others we need first to create these feelings towards ourselves. Enter your own state of meditation and become aware of your heart. Allow yourself to feel deserving of love. Allow yourself to surrender to this feeling. Imagine that you cradle a new-born child in your arms. The child is you. Let loving feelings flow through you, let the child be held in a deep and safe embrace. Offer love to yourself first until you feel nourished. This meditation appears to be very simple but it is quite likely to reveal how we have been loved in the past.

When you feel ready and able to generate this feeling towards others, you can extend your loving thoughts to others. It is natural to extend love first to loved ones, but radiating love in this way need have no boundaries or limitations. The daily news brings us face to face with grim reality and the despair of the many. Hold these in your loving thoughts and discover the meaning of the global human family. There is an old saying 'energy follows thought'.

The Way of the Bodhisattva

Whatever merit I may have obtained, may I become thereby the soother of every pain for all living beings. The merits which I have acquired in all my rebirths through

thoughts, words and deeds, all this I am giving away
without regard to myself, in order to realize the salvation
of all living beings.

Vow of the Bodhisattva

It is one thing to bear others in mind as best we can as we go
about our daily business and ordinary lives, it is quite another
matter to make the happiness of all others the central,
overriding and ultimate concern of our existence. Yet this is the
way of the **Bodhisattva**. Osho illustrates the great compassion
of the Bodhisattva in his own inimitable style through a story:

A story is told that Buddha reached the doors of the
ultimate, **nirvana**. The doors were opened, the angels
were dancing and singing to receive him – because it
rarely happens in millions of years that a human being
becomes a Buddha. Those doors open, and that day is
naturally a great day of celebration. All the ancient
Buddhas had gathered, and there was great rejoicing and
flowers were showering and music was played, and
everything was decorated – it was a day of celebration.

But the Buddha did not enter the door. And the ancient
Buddhas, all with folded hands, asked him, requested him
to come in: 'Why is he standing outside?' And Buddha is
reported to have said, 'Unless all others who are coming
behind me enter, I am not going to enter. I will keep
myself outside because once I come in then I disappear
then I will not be of any help to these people. I see
millions of people stumbling and groping in the dark. I
myself began groping in the same way for millions of lives
I would like to give them my hand. Please close the door.
When everybody has come I myself will knock, then you
can receive me.'[6]

Here is the path of transcendent becoming. In the exchange of
self for others, who can fail to see the similarity between the
Way of the Bodhisattva and the Christian ideal? Carrying others
is the ultimate path of the heart. This is the meaning of the
Greater Vehicle, which is **Mahayana** Buddhism in contrast to
the Lesser Vehicle, which is **Hinayana** Buddhism. The Greater
Vehicle holds all, the Lesser Vehicle holds the individual. Such
high ideals appear impossible from the perspective of the ego.
The all-encompassing concerns for the self keep us pinioned to
our own perceived requirements. Mahayana Buddhism offers
many deep exercises and meditations to counter the voice of the
small self. Both analytical meditations and meditations of

concentration are used. Together, these meditations foster the birth of equanimity, create a deep understanding of our dependence on others and replace self-cherishing with the cherishing of others. Such practices give birth to the **bodhi mind**, the awakened mind, and culminate in the supreme aspiration, which is taking responsibility for all beings. When the supreme aspiration is as natural as the breath itself, the Bodhisattva intent is born. The following words represent the vows and offerings made on this particular path:

> Whatever there may be found in the world: flowers, fruits, vegetables, and the life-giving waters; the mountains of precious stone, the forest-solitudes for meditation, the creepers adorned with beautiful radiant blossoms, the trees whose twigs are bent under the burden of delicious fruit, the perfumes and scents from the world of gods, the miraculous trees, the jewel-trees, the lovely ponds of lotus-flowers, echoing with sweet song of swans, the wild-growing plants as well as those of the fields: everything that is suitable as an offering and all that is contained in the infinity of space and does not belong to anybody; I collect all this in my mind and offer it to the Perfect Ones and their spiritual sons.

The next step brings a complete surrender.

> Wholely and without reserve I dedicate myself to the Enlightened Ones and their spiritual sons: Take possession of me, exalted beings! Fill me with humility. I offer myself as your servant. Having become your property, I have nothing more to fear in this world. I will do only what is helpful to other beings. I will give up my former wrong-doings and not commit further misdeeds. Due to hatred and infatuation I have committed many wrong deeds. I did not realize that I am only a traveller, passing through this world. Day and night without cessation vitality decreases and death approaches. This very day, therefore I will take my refuge in the great and powerful protectors of the world. From the bottom of my heart I take my refuge in the doctrine – and likewise in the multitude of Bodhisattvas. With folded hands I implore the Perfect Enlightened Ones in all the regions of the universe: may they kindle the light of truth for all those who on account of their delusion would otherwise fall into the abyss of misery.[7]

Through this path, we see a living tradition that places the heart at its very centre. Do not think the way of the heart can be confined to any single process. Buddhism has merely articulated a particular route that renders the process of transformation visible. The path of the heart has taken numerous incarnations. Sufi mystics know the opened heart brings ecstacy. Christian mystics find the love of God here. The living experience of the heart is what matters. The name for the experience is no more than a label. Do not think that the mystical love of the heart is somehow beyond reach. When you find your heart's desire, the heart will flower.

EXERCISE 5.5 THE WORLD IN MY HEART

Sit in meditation and hold an image of the world as viewed from space. Place the image of the world in your heart. That is all you need do. Your love for the world will do the rest.

06

being: the creative response

In this chapter you will learn:
- to discover your creativity through meditation
- to see with the mind's eye
- about the symbolism of the mandala.

The power of the creative imagination is not merely content with observing the world as it is, accepting a given reality, but is capable of creating a new reality by transforming the inner as well as the outerworld.

Lama Govinda, *Creative Meditation*

The creative mind

Children create continuously through play and imagination. They are not inhibited by self-consciousness or hampered by doubting criticism. They simply create. This openness to each new experience is not unlike the openness of the meditative mind. When we are open to each moment, we can receive and we can create. Neither the creativity of the child nor the creativity of the meditative mind gives rise to artistic endeavour that seeks public approval and acclaim. This is creativity for its own sake that seeks no further recognition. Meditation awakens the mind as a whole. As the mind is awakened it responds through creativity, which is a natural function. It is a sad fact that the creative instinct rarely survives the passage into adult life. The playful and imaginative child grows up and puts down childish things. Spontaneous creativity is lost amid adolescent angst and finally extinguished by both the burdens and distractions of adult life. Though a minority will manage to keep the creative light alive, for the majority, the time for creative expression is over. Ask yourself, in what ways do you express your own creativity? What value do you place on personal creative expression. What is preventing you from being creative? Are you just too busy in life to find a space for yourself? Do you feel that you lack creative ability?

The new technology at our disposal opens up creative possibilities and opportunities never seen before in the history of this planet. Computer technology is creative technology. Here are new tools to feed the imagination and inspire the mind. Don't hang back. Here is a brand new way of expressing yourself. Creativity can never be limited to any one form, it just springs unbounded from life itself. Every society has expressed itself through its creative endeavours. The utilitarian and the liturgical, the mundane and the sacred, the performing arts and the visual arts, works great and small, all are the outpourings of the human mind seeking to translate the human experience. The human imagination knows no limits. The imaginings of one generation so often become the reality of the next. So let us celebrate human creativity in its broadest forms and look forward with great anticipation to the new creative forms that will arise as technological creativity comes into its own.

We undervalue the creative imagination at our collective peril. It is both normal and significant. Through imagination we can stand in another's shoes. We can empathize with a stranger. We can transcend the physical limitations of time and space. We can create. We can envision and inspire. Innovation and invention take root from the imagination. Great works of the imagination come to have a reality of their own. The worlds created by Tolkein or Gene Rodenberry began only in the minds of these creators but have now become mythic landscapes shared by the many. However, the imagination does not belong solely to the world of children – it is only abandoned in favour of the intellect and to our cost. Though it is easy to think of the imagination as no more than pretence or make-believe, the imagination has a deeper significance. Far from seeing the imagination as a peripheral quality, Brian Lancaster, a senior lecturer in psychology , concludes that, 'Imagination thus lies right at the heart of the nature of mind.'[1] We should take this viewpoint seriously if we care seriously about human potential.

The breath of inspiration

Inspiration is the very heart, the central force of all meditation. But since inspiration is a spontaneous facility, it cannot be created on command, but only induced by arousing our interest or our admiration. Thus, before we can get inspired, we must prepare the ground.

Lama Govinda, *Creative Meditation*

Inspiration remains enigmatic, even to the artist. It may come as a moment of heightened awareness, a fleeting vision, or a deep but momentary impression. The word spirit is derived from the Latin *inspirare*, which means 'to breathe'. Inspiration is as subtle and invisible as the breath. Coleridge called the imagination 'a repetition in the finite mind of the eternal act of creation of the infinite I AM'. In other words he likened the personal creativity of the artist to the cosmic palette of the Creator. This may seem to be an extreme sentiment that detracts from the innate creativity of the individual. Yet biographical accounts of creative individuals often reveal that inspiration is experienced as a revelation. It feels as if something is being received, not generated. Coleridge himself wrote the epic poem 'Kubla Khan' as a result of a dream. Having fallen asleep while reading about a Mogul emperor, he awoke in receipt of a whole poem. Robert Louis Stevenson said that much of his writing was developed by 'little people' in his dreams. The German chemist F.A. Kekule attributed his breakthrough with the benzene molecule to a dream in which he saw a snake with its tail in its mouth. The author J.B. Priestly described his own creative experiences, which led him to write *Man and Time*. He felt he had touched something close to a mystical experience, which released him from 'an egocentric relation with passing time'. Feeling outside time and personality, Priestly was turned into 'a creator, working like a man possessed, lending me energy and imagination and a creative will'.[2]

It is easy to see the creativity of the great names in literature, theatre, music and the arts. It seems difficult to find this same current in our own lives. We need first to change our mindset – creativity is possible and creativity is the natural activity of the awakened mind. Lama Govinda offers wise and eloquent advice:

> All of us could be more creative if we would think less of the doings and achievements of our mundane life, of our personalities and our ambitions – if we thought more of the hidden forces and faculties within ourselves. We make programs with our brains instead of using the ever present forces of our heart. We cheat ourselves with our coarse plans and trivial aims. We do not see what is nearest to us, we do not hear the whispering voices of our heart because of the noise of our words. Our eyes are blinded by the glaring colours of daylight. Our restless life takes away our breath, our insatiable desires make our heart palpitate and cause our blood to race through the veins. Thus we do not hear the sound of other spheres, do not see the great visions, do not feel the mysterious vibrations – and the eternal stream flows past us unto the infinite from whence it came.[3]

Here is a plea for the open heart and the open mind. Here is a call for moments of quiet. Here is a cry to rise above the trivial and the mundane, the personality and the immediate. Here is the prompt to look within. Here is the challenge to awaken the mind through the meditative life. Here is the opportunity to find your own creative wellspring.

Sacred art

> Painting is meditation for me. As soon as I pick up the brush, there is no difference from meditation.
> Okbong Sunim, *Walking on Lotus Flowers*

It is no coincidence that the great meditative traditions of the world have also become rich artistic traditions. Architecture, statuary, painting, metal work, carving, casting, brush work, weaving and much more have all become part of a sacred iconography. Every tradition has expressed its experience through art of some kind. Close to home and on a small scale we can see the impact of in-depth spiritual work upon creativity through the artistic heritage of the Golden Dawn. The Hermetic Order of Golden Dawn, which formed in 1886, took its *raison d'être* from the living current of the Western spiritual tradition and proceeded to respond to its own revelation and received wisdom. This brief flowering dug deep into Celtic, Egyptian and Hermetic symbolism. It revived ancient interests and represented the symbols of the past in a fresh guise. The symbols of the Tarot were revivified here. Sacred drama in the initiatory tradition of the ancient world was restored. In the temple the creative arts were revitalized as colour and symbol took on a spiritual significance. Creativity flowed from the temple into the outer world through literature, scholarly works and esoteric teachings. In this brief historical moment we see the same principles that have nourished the great traditions. Flowing outwards from the spiritual centre, artistic and creative endeavours express, restate and present the moment of revelation through solid form. Unlike the great traditions, which rest upon the firm foundation of the centuries, the Golden Dawn was a seed planted in unfamiliar territory. But its legacy lives on.

There is a significant but subtle difference between secular and sacred art. The first is designed to be viewed from the outside and the second is viewed from the inside. Secular art may or may not carry a message for the viewer, whereas a deeper message is invariably embedded in spiritual art. Tibetan Buddhism offers a very particular approach to its many paintings and mandalas. The beholder enters the picture as a participant. The work of art is internally recreated by the beholder down to the last detail until it stands before inner vision. Finally, ever faithful to Buddhist teaching, the beholder reverses the creative process by dissolving the vision. Here is a concept quite outside the common Western experience of artistic enjoyment. In the Tibetan tradition it is even intended that the beholder should re-experience the vision of the artist. This relationship between the original artist, the work of art and the beholder is quite unique. It is incomprehensible in purely secular terms. When artistic expression is personal, the viewer is free to draw personal conclusions and interpretations. Sacred art expresses the universal through the particular. The beholder and the creator may touch the same vision. Such a deep relationship to a work of art is only made possible through the milieu in which it has arisen. Meditation techniques train the mind to create and dissolve images in the mind's eye. It then becomes quite natural to enter the world of a painting.

In the West such experiences belong only to the world of fairy-tale and children's literature; adults might learn a great deal from the openness of a child's imagination. The writer C.S. Lewis knew much about the spiritual power of the active imagination. Along with J.R.R. Tolkein and Charles Williams, he was the third member of the self-styled group known as The Inklings. These three writers consciously evoked the creative imagination of the popular mind with enormous impact. C.S. Lewis constantly employed techniques to encourage the active imagination. In the children's story *Voyage of the Dawn Treader* the reader is invited to enter a magical world through a picture:

> Eustace rushed towards the picture. Edmund, who knew something about magic, sprang after him, warning him to look out and not be a fool. Lucy grabbed at him from the other side and was dragged forward. And by this time either they had grown much smaller or the picture had grown bigger. Eustace jumped, tried to pull it off the wall and found himself standing on the frame; in front of him was not glass but real sea, and wind and waves rushing up to the frame as they might a rock.[4]

Like Lama Govinda, C.S. Lewis also knew that, 'A spiritual discipline or meditational practice which shuns the power of imagination deprives itself of the most effective and vital means of transforming human nature as it is into what it could be'.[5] Lewis' books, for both children and adults, live through the creative imagination. Lewis wrote about the reality of spiritual transformation, not through heady theological doctrine, but through our deepest symbolic vocabulary. Locating the openness of a childlike imagination is not difficult but it asks for honesty and simplicity. Watching children in imaginative play takes us towards our own imagination again. There are many opportunities to see as a child again.

This is not the childish exercise it might appear to be, but a first step towards utilizing the imagination under conscious control.

EXERCISE 6.1 CHILD'S PLAY

Find a copy of a painting or picture that you have previously enjoyed looking at. Instead of merely observing the image as an outsider, allow the image to come to life in the mind's eye. First have the image in front of you. Spend some time becoming familiar with it and pay attention to the details. When you are ready, close your eyes and attempt to reproduce the image in your imagination. When the picture is clear, take a leap of the imagination and find yourself stepping through the frame into the image. Once within the landscape attempt to employ all your senses and explore the scene as it is represented. When you wish to leave, mentally step back through the frame then watch the image settle and become flat once more. Finally allow the image to dissolve in the mind's eye.

Seeing with the mind's eye

> The power of forming clear cut mental images is essential to progress in meditation.
>
> Christmas Humphreys, *Concentration and Meditation*

Imagination begins with the image-making facility of the mind, often called the mind's eye. This is a normal but underdeveloped ability. The mass bombardment of external visual images has served to dampen the active imagination and make us lazy. The imagination is a much underrated mental force. We have become so used to thinking in words instead. The writer Henry Skolimowski clearly understands the value of the creative imagination:

> The power of visualization is the power of the mind. It is a form of day-dreaming which through a strange alchemy that occurs between the mind and reality, can transform imagination into reality. How this happens is a bit of a mystery but there are many important things that we do not know, we should cherish and celebrate mystery rather than be afraid of it.[6]

Guided meditations, which employ the power to visualize images, have become increasingly popular recently. Such meditations most often take the form of directed journeys through inner symbolic landscapes. Employing this natural function regularly awakens the active imagination and brings creativity in its wake. Childlike imagination meets adult awareness in a creative fusion of ideas and possibilities; this is the opening of the mind's eye.

EXERCISE 6.2 LOOK AROUND

Stop what you are doing. Look around. Open the inner eye. What do you see in your immediate surroundings? Spend several minutes just observing your surroundings. What do you notice? There should be plenty to see: colour, shape, texture, contrast, light and shade surround us constantly. Get used to looking wherever you find yourself.

How observant are you? The mind's eye is directly related to the seeing eye. If you sleepwalk through life, the mind's eye will have little to draw upon. The creative imagination, which fuels visualization, draws naturally upon memory or pure imagination. In other words images can be created within the mind from solid experience or conjured from the realms of fantasy. Asked to create moonlight over water or a tree on an autumnal day, how do you fare? When the mind's eye is open, we see everyday life with new eyes. How often do we feel that our life has become bogged down. We repeat the same routines, go through the same sequences, follow the same habits, maybe even have the same thoughts over and over again. When we are in the doldrums, we instinctively want a change of scene, we hanker after the new and the different. However, even the new will become old, the novelty will tire and the doldrums will return. Much of life is routine, humdrum and repetitive. What we need is not a change of scene but a change of inner perspective: 'Change your awareness and you live in a different world, experience a different reality.'[7]

It is no secret that particular mind-altering drugs produce a new, if temporary, perspective. The intensity of this sudden shift in awareness often astounds; creativity occurs quite spontaneously. The world is seen through new eyes, even the most mundane and ordinary take on an extraordinary quality. The very basis of perception shifts as the narrow boundaries of the five senses are dismantled. Individuals down the ages have known of the mind-expanding properties of plants and substances. However, during the 1960s the secret of the few became the property of the masses and psychedelic art, music and youth culture rose on the back of widespread mind expansion. The perspective and perception of a generation was changed. This was a revolution in consciousness. Meditation also produces a change of perspective and perception. However, this shift of awareness is not temporary but permanent, not fleeting but stable. The meditative mind is established gently. It is built from within. The meditative mind is the creative mind. Open the inner eye, which is the eye of vision. Awaken the creative imagination by utilizing your image-making facility in the most ordinary circumstances.

As we make a conscious effort to develop the ability to visualize images, we are drawing on the functions of the right hemisphere of the brain, which is responsible for pattern recognition and the comprehension of symbols. Clinical studies with split-brain patients, in whom the *corpus callosum* has been severed, are thought provoking. The left hemisphere of the brain interprets, rationalizes and justifies what the right hemisphere is showing. This major function has led to the left hemisphere being called the interpreter. A typical experiment with split-brain patients shows the interpreter at work. When the command 'walk' was flashed to the right hemisphere alone, the subject immediately stood up to leave the test area and rationalized the action by explaining, 'I'm going into the house to get a coke.' This justification fulfilled the instruction. In another experiment, when gruesome images were displayed to the right hemisphere alone, an unknown sense of fear was projected momentarily. The subject suddenly expressed a fear of the doctor. These studies reveal a curious state of affairs, in which the right hemisphere knows what is being experienced but does not speak for itself, except through the language of symbols, patterns and recognition. The left hemisphere surmises what is being experienced and, having control over the function of speech, presents its own hypothesis as fact. Further experiments suggest that final explanation of any experience lies with the left hemisphere of the brain. In other words, 'what we experience is the output of the interpreter'.[8]

In a rare condition known as Capgras syndrome, which follows particular damage to the right side of the brain, patients believe that family and friends are imposters. The researchers Ramachandran and Hirstein suggest that although the brain recognizes the face in the inferior temporal cortex, physical damage prevents emotional recognition in the limbic system. In other words, the left brain recognizes the face but, in the absence of an emotional trigger, rationalizes that it belongs not to a real loved one but rather to an imposter![9] It is no wonder then that all meditation systems seek to bypass this intellectual function, which will simply rationalize any two pieces of information. The dominance of the left-hand brain can be reduced by techniques that simultaneously quieten the interpreter by empowering the imagination. The interpreting function exercised by the left hemisphere, however, can be put to good use when it falls under the control of a higher centre. The researchers Bogen and Bogen have argued that creativity depends on the integration of hemispheric function. Meditation brings an observable integration of the two hemispheres. Monitoring devices such as the Mind Mirror reveal this activity very clearly. When the two hemispheres work together, the right hemisphere generates flashes of insight, while the left hemisphere provides analytical scrutiny.[10]

Visualization is widely used in both Eastern and Western systems, with the possible exception of Zen, which employs no images. When using this approach an image is created and held in the mind. Simple images progress towards more complex ones as the meditator gains in experience. It is important to realize that visualization is not the purpose of any given meditation, but it is only the means to this end. Visualization is the vehicle of the realization, not the realization itself. In other words, we create images internally in order to precipitate insight, not to create a succession of images. To reproduce an image in the mind's eye is only a matter of technique. The vital aspect of the meditation lies in the personal response to the image. The seeds of transformation lie in this most sacred of spaces, in between the traditional image and the personal response to it. At first, visualized images often feel artificial and can appear to be flat and two-dimensional. Concentration may flag and the image falters. However, with practice the two-dimensional image comes to life, a landscape can be entered and explored and an inner world has been created.

When this facility is developed during periods of meditation, it begins to function spontaneously outside formal meditation sessions. The imagination, the image-making function, springs to life. Moreover, the visual senses, both internal and external, become very sharp. The eye of the mind becomes active. Everyday occurrences are quietly observed. It becomes natural to notice subtle differences of colour, the play of light and shade, shapes, textures and the whole host of varied nuances that provide the backdrop to ordinary life. No effort is required, this detached observation just happens when the mind is alive. This extra dimension bridges the outer world of events, situations and locations with the inner world of subjective responses. The resulting creative fusion brings the ability to express both the external and the internal world in meaningful ways.

The inner world: the mandala

The mandala is like a map of the world, which we want to explore and realize in the great venture which is meditation.

Lama Govinda, *Creative Meditation*

A map represents the outer world. We are familiar with its symbols. This symbolic representation enables us to journey in the outer world. The mandala is a map of the inner world. If we wish to travel in the inner world, we need to become familiar with the symbolism of the specialized map. It is a mistake to view a mandala purely as a work of art; it is a piece of sacred art with a specific intent. The mandala has been described as 'a geometric projection of the world reduced to an essential pattern'.[11] Although mandalas have evolved within different traditions, the same principle applies. Art expresses a precise and particular symbolic language, which has been codified through centuries of meditative experience. Images and symbols resonate with the vocabulary of the psyche; words alone do not touch these deeper levels of being. This is the essential difference between the sacred and the mundane. Sacred art is never idiosyncratic but universal, never random but precise. It appeals not to the senses but to the soul, not to the eye but to the awakened mind.

In the specialized language of the sacred, every detail of colour and composition has a place and purpose. The mandala takes the circle as its form and may contain further concentric circles. The central point has special significance, lines radiate from this point and cut the circle into four cardinal segments. A square commonly surrounds the central point, creating further triangular areas. The basic geometric forms of circle, square and triangle are endlessly elaborated. Within the area of the mandala, the four cardinal directions are often marked with gates. The architectural images lend themselves naturally to an inner landscape. The different areas take on symbolic scenic qualities, such as gardens in paradise, courtyards and chambers. The mandala becomes a palace or a representation of the ideal city where the individual undertakes a journey to the centre.

The ability to enter the realm of the mandala clearly depends upon the ability to bring it to life in the mind. The structure of the mandala is fixed in the mind before the meditation proceeds. To the observer the mandala remains no more than a two-dimensional image. To the active participant the mandala becomes an inner world that comes to life through meditation. In Tantric Buddhism the mandala is approached through the East, the place of sunrise. The journey through the inner landscape follows the prescribed route to the centre, which is both the human heart and the axis of the universe. The mandala is the universal temple on top of the sacred mountain. The four cardinal directions orient the participants to time and space. Divine figures are encountered at the appropriate points. Guardians stand at significant thresholds to offer traditional challenges and test the traveller.

Jung rediscovered the significance of the mandala form for himself. In 1916 he had instinctively painted a mandala, but without understanding its significance. Some two years later the impulse to draw mandala forms returned. This time he experienced a conscious realization of their significance. He wrote, 'Only gradually did I discover what the mandala really is: Formation, Transformation, Eternal Mind's eternal recreation.'[12] Here is an eternal truth known by other names. For the Buddhist this is Impermanence. For the Western Mysteries this is Transformation. For the emerging current of ecological spirituality: Everything Changes. Jung had to rediscover what had never been lost in unbroken spiritual traditions. Tibetan Buddhism makes extensive use of the mandala form. The ceremonial Navajo sand paintings are mandalas. Hinduism has retained the sacred circle. The West had destroyed its own knowledge of sacred forms with the rise of an intellectually based orthodoxy. In new times new mandalas will arise.

A Western mandala

Mandalas are birth places, vessels of birth in the most literal sense.

Carl G. Jung, *The Structure and Dynamics of the Psyche*

This meditation is written in the form of an interior journey. It calls upon the full range of imaginative faculties. Calling upon these inner senses brings the images to life. This journey takes the form of a visit to a sacred place. This location signifies the sacred place in the centre of being, which is represented by the mandala. We designate the sacred space by treading out the circle. We acknowledge the four cardinal points and finally focus upon the centre of the mandala.

If you would like to undertake this journey, first become familiar with the inner landscape by reading the text several times. As preparation, first decide on the form of inner landscape in which you feel comfortable. You might resonate to the dynamics of a medieval cathedral, an ancient temple, a small sanctuary or even to a wide open space on a moonlit night. When you are ready to commence the meditation begin to create the scenes inwardly in your mind. Create the scene slowly and fully in your mind and then simply find yourself as part of the scene. Each of the sequences you undertake will evoke a personal response from you.

EXERCISE 6.3 THE INNER TEMPLE

Sit in meditation and begin to build your chosen scene through your imagination. Find yourself standing in the sacred place that you have designated. Let your first act be the walking of a circle in a clockwise direction. Make this as large or as small as you wish. As you walk this first circle designate four points, one at each quarter to represent the cardinal directions east, south, west and north. Complete your first circuit. Undertake a second circuit and stop briefly at each of the quarters earlier designated. At each quarter use a symbolic gesture to acknowledge the cardinal direction. You could offer a salute, extend both arms, even mentally draw a sign. Repeat this at each quarter. Undertake a third and final circuit. As you walk this third circle, forge a trail of golden light as you walk. When your circuit is complete step into the circle and go to the central point. In the central place, imagine a shaft of light stretching upwards into the heavens and down into the heart of the earth. Enter deep meditation here. When you are ready to close your meditation, first allow the central light to fade and dissolve. From your central position turn to each of the quarters in reverse order and allow all images to dissolve. Next permit the golden circle to fade in the reverse order to which it was constructed.

When your inner journey is completed, you might like to write a brief report for yourself. Then try representing your experience in another medium altogether. Translate your feelings, memories and actions into a non-verbal form as a statement. The sacred moment, no matter how brief, has always been the seed for the creativity of the soul.

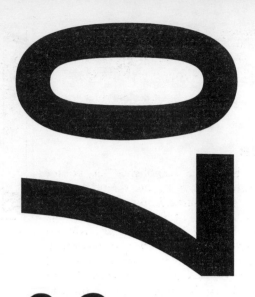

07

doing: the way of activity

In this chapter you will learn:
- about ecological spirituality
- about Zen archery
- about dance as meditation
- about the spiritual garden
- to build a shrine.

Trivial participation ultimately bores you, leaves behind a sense of shallowness, contributes little to your deeper sense of life. Significant participation, on the other hand, engages you, enthrals and satisfies you, it contributes to the meaning of your life.

Henry Skolimowski, *EcoYoga*

The integrated life

Once the meditative mind has been established, it is not confined to a particular posture or place. Rather the meditative mind is continuously present. It will suffuse mundane activities and transform the everyday into meditative practice. In the words of Ani Tenzin Palmo, 'Practice is something you do moment to moment, all through the day. It is the way you relate to the people you meet. It is the way you drink your tea, approach your work and how you become more aware of your internal responses to things.'[1] When the so-called mundane and the so-called spiritual merge into a seamless garment, there is just the One Life sanctified and made meaningful. Our difficulty in reconciling the spiritual with the material reflects the deep split that still exists in Western philosophy. Only holistic philosophy finds no gap between these two poles; holistic philosophy upholds the integration of opposites and affirms interconnectedness.

Holistic spirituality is not new but its time has come once more as we labour under the dead hand of materialism. Pythagoras is best remembered for his mathematical theorem, yet his philosophy went far beyond mathematics. He established a school of philosophy in the tradition of the mystery schools of ancient Egypt where he spent some 22 years. During this time it seems very clear that he became deeply immersed in the long established spirituality of Egypt. Here was a rich holistic current where priests were also astronomers, architects and healers and where priestesses were sacred dancers and musicians. Wisdom was both practical and moral, cosmic and earthly. Egyptian metaphysics encompassed the movements of the heavens as well as the movement of stone. Here was a spirituality that embraced the skies above and the earth below in a sweeping and magnificent unity expressed through the many languages of the sciences and the arts. It was this model that inspired Pythagoras. He adopted and adapted the sacred teaching of the Mystery School and created them anew in Greece.

Centuries later the English philosopher Roger Bacon was inspired once more to lay the foundations for a holistic philosophy. Bacon called his schema the Great Instauration. This grand scheme sought nothing less than the universal and general reformation of the whole wide world through the renewal of all arts and sciences. He represented his schema by a model that he called the Pyramid of Philosophy. Each face represented one of the three aspects of philosophy – divine, human and natural. Additionally, the Pyramid of Philosophy was divided into three tiers. The base represented history, which Bacon called Experience through Action. The middle stage represented physics, which he called Material Causes. The third stage represented metaphysics, known as Final Causes. In this model, the arts and the sciences were related to the Divine. Bacon's hopes for a spiritual philosophy find an echo in contemporary language. He too wanted to bring 'light-bringing' thoughts and 'light-bringing' experiences. Pythagoras left little as a written legacy, but Bacon left much for succeeding generations to ponder upon. Both men were inspired by a vision of an integrated life. Bacon placed much emphasis on the imaginative arts and Pythagoras placed much emphasis on number. Within a holistic framework every part can reveal the whole. Holism speaks to us again today; we again seek out the integrated life. The activities of life become the warp and the weft that sustain the unity of mind, body and soul. Activity becomes meditation, meditation becomes activity.

At the time in which we now live spiritual action is of the utmost value. In 1993 His Holiness the Dalai Lama gave the closing address for the World Parliament of Religions. This assembly was convened to discuss the global problems facing the world community. The theme of his closing address was the call to personal action. This was a request to act in the material world from a spiritual position. Here was a call to unity of thought and action, the full integration of the spiritual with the material, meditation in action. When spiritual thought and material action are united we participate in life and partake of life.

Ecological spirituality

What the universe is depends on you; treat it like a machine and it becomes a machine; treat it like a divine place and it becomes a divine place.

Henry Skolimowski, *EcoYoga*

The Way of Activity is the natural complement to the Way of Contemplation. Activity is the extension of awareness, an expression of choice and a statement of clear motivation. In this way, life takes on a single focus and sharp direction through word and deed, thought and action. The inner life cannot be separated from its outer expression. When we have experienced a deep connection to others and the greater world, it is impossible to deny this truth. Once we have seen the invisible threads that bind everything together it is impossible to act as an isolated being. Changes in consciousness bring changes in action. Meditation brings an expansion of consciousness. As consciousness expands we become aware of the greater currents at work in the world today. Once we have awoken to ecological spirituality we can only accept the responsibilities that understanding brings. We have no option but to act accordingly.

Henry Skolimowski holds the chair of Ecological Philosophy at the University of Warsaw in Poland. He is the founder of Eco-Philosophy, a practical–spiritual holistic philosophy that addresses the needs of our times. Like many other spiritual voices of today, he calls for participation in the world, not escape from it. In his book, *EcoYoga*, he takes Yoga into a new arena. He envisages the world as a sanctuary to be approached with reverence. He reminds us that this idea is itself empowering, so take the image into daily life and discover what your role is in the sanctuary of the world. He offers meditations that are experienced through life itself. His meditations are those that bring us into closer contact with the landscape, with trees, rocks and running water. He reminds us to walk in beauty. He urges us to realize our own potential. He asks us to remember the main focus of EcoYoga – grace, health and hope. The meditations he offers are simple and gentle, life affirming and reverential. He too gives us integrated meditation, spiritual thought and dynamic action. Skolimowski writes: 'A deep comprehension of ecology is reverence in action. This reverence is a form of spirituality. In our times the ecological and the spiritual become one. This is the foundation of ecological spirituality.' He continues, 'Healing the planet and ourselves is spiritual work of the first magnitude in our day and age. Who can deny the truth of this statement. Whatever may be our race and religion, ecology binds us all together. Ecology is the universal religious project of our times.'[2] Here is the way of activity that beckons us all. It was the Greeks who called the earth Gaia. This name has become a rallying call for all who love the world, so in your meditation call her name too.

EXERCISE 7.1 CALLING GAIA

This meditation will be so much stronger if you can be outside in nature. Just settle into your chosen spot and first look at everything around you. Look with your eyes and also reflect on all the processes of Nature, which are going on in every plant and blade of grass. Close your eyes and allow your mind to move beyond your immediate spot into the realm of Nature herself. Begin to hum her name slowly, repeating it over. Let your vision of the world expand until you project your mind into space and see the planet from afar. Call Gaia all the while and see her form in the planet itself. Feel that your mind is returning towards the earth, your home. Allow yourself to feel like a child in your mother's arms as you open your eyes and once again see the face of Nature.

Ecological spirituality has a real significance and meaning. This is no esoteric byway but a broad and rewarding path. The issues that face the world at this time are global. Ecology knows no national boundaries. Gaia is the world itself. This is a much needed universal image for a common humanity. Your meditations upon Gaia will lead you into a unique relationship. Earth wisdom comes to those who live close to nature but industrialization has rendered us proud and forgetful. Skolimowski acknowledges the significance of this newly remembered spiritual path: 'Thus a new religion is emerging, the religion which follows from the yoga of reverence for Mother Earth. Its church is the entire Cosmos.'[3] Here is the way of activity, which is relevant for today and tomorrow.

By contrast to the way of ecological spirituality, which is open to all, certain paths of action have developed into specialized and arcane avenues. Zen archery remains a way of activity for the very few. The dogmatic might seek to debate the shared value in such obscure preoccupations. Zen archery is nevertheless a fascinating example. The spiritual and the physical merge to create a unique form of expression.

Zen archery

The man, the art, the work – it's all one.

Eugene Herrigel, *Zen in the Art of Archery*

The classic book, *Zen in the Art of Archery*, provides a glimpse into a world rarely seen by Westerners. It is a personal tale, simply told, of a European's encounter with Zen through archery. Like all good tales, this one is worth retelling. In the 1930s a professor of philosophy at Tokyo University wistfully hoped to be admitted into Zen. As a Westerner he was an outsider. No doors were opened willingly for him. It was finally suggested that he might be permitted to enter indirectly through one of the associated arts. The possibilities included painting, flower arranging and archery. The professor, Eugene Herrigel, chose archery and was finally accepted as a student to a renowned Master Kenzo Awa; his path into Zen had begun.

From the outset, Herrigel makes it clear that archery is neither sport nor competition but the 'artless art', a religious ritual in its own right. He describes archery in the language of paradox: 'Spiritual exercises ... whose aim consists in hitting a spiritual goal, so that fundamentally the marksman aims at himself and may even succeed in hitting himself.' He summarizes archery with concepts unfamiliar to the Western mind:

> It is necessary for the archer to become, in spite of himself, an unmoved centre. Then comes the supreme and ultimate miracle: art becomes 'artless', shooting becomes not-shooting, a shooting without bow and arrow; the teacher becomes a pupil again, the Master a beginner, the end a beginning, and the beginning perfection.

It is clear that, although Herrigel heard these same words, their meaning eluded him. Herrigel's apprenticeship with his teacher was long and hard. After a year's work, he had learned only to draw the bow. Although body and breath moved as one in a series of rhythmic movements, there was much more still to learn. Loosening the arrow brought weeks and months of fruitless effort. Herrigel was baffled by the Master's instructions: 'The shot will only go smoothly when it takes the archer by surprise. It must be as if the bowstring suddenly cut through the thumb that held it. You mustn't open the right hand on purpose.' Herrigel's continuing failures were a source of great confusion and distress while he continued to apply a logical consciousness to the problem: 'I draw the bow and loose the shot in order to hit the target.' The Master presented only paradox: 'The more obstinately you try to learn how to shoot an arrow for the sake of hitting the goal, the less you will succeed in the one and the further the other will recede.' Far from being encouraged to practise loosing the shot, Herrigel, in common with other students, was instructed to practise only the quality of self-detached immersion in all daily affairs. Frustrated by failure, Herrigel sought to achieve the desired smooth release through a technical solution: releasing the pressure of the fingers over the thumb at the appropriate moment. Proud of the result, Herrigel was pleased to demonstrate the resulting shot. The Master watched in silence, took the bow from Herrigel's hands, turned and sat with his back to the woebegone student. Herrigel had tried to cheat. He had attempted to reduce the artless art to mere technique. His training was over.

It was only after much persuasion that Herrigel was readmitted. He had already spent four years in training and could not yet loose an arrow in the Zen spirit. Herrigel continued to practise. Then one day, after a shot, the Master made a deep bow: 'It shot,' he announced. A breakthrough had been made. At last Herrigel became able to distinguish the right shots from the failures, the purposeless aim from the contrived. Though he had now clearly entered the artless art up to this point, he had received no instruction about hitting the target. At last Master Kenzo Awa was willing to engage in this stage too. Once again Herrigel encountered the paradox he had come to expect: 'Put the thought of hitting right out of your mind and you can be a master even if every shot does not hit. The hits on the target are only the outward proof and confirmation of your purposelessness, at its highest of your egolessness, your self-abandonment.' Further comment was forthcoming: 'Your arrows do not carry because they do not reach far enough spiritually. A good archer can shoot further than with a medium-strong bow than an unspiritual teacher can with the strongest.' Herrigel did indeed learn to hit the target in the spirit of the tradition. Finally, after six years, Herrigel had been initiated into the artless art, not of archery but of self-mastery. All the time the journey seemed outward but the real transformation took place inwardly, its measure being reflected outwardly. Herrigel was changed by the Great Doctrine. At the close of the book we hear the words of Master Kenzo Awa:

> I must warn you one thing. You have become a different person in the course of these years for this is what archer means: a profound far-reaching contest of the archer with himself ... You will see with others' eyes and measure with other measures. It has happened to me too and it happens to all who are touched by the spirit of this art.[4]

The same principles have been embedded in swordsmanship as sacred art. Success comes with 'presence of heart, neither knowledge nor technique'. Here too the pupil must become 'egoless and purposeless'. Accordingly perfection is reached,

'When the heart is no more troubled by no more thoughts of I and you, of the opponent, of one's own sword, no more thoughts even of life and death. All is emptiness: your own self, the flashing sword and the arms that wield it. Even the thought of emptiness is no longer there.' The Great Doctrine moulds itself to innumerable vehicles. Calligraphy, painting and even the gentle art of flower arranging have expressed the same truth.

The cosmic dance

The dance opens a door in the soul to divine influences.

Sultan Walad

People have danced together since the earliest times. The imprints of stamping feet have been found in Neolithic caves when dance probably brought the group together in celebration, triumph or sorrow. Movement is intimately connected with human emotion. Dance naturally lends itself to deep expression – the body speaks in movement, the steps speak through rhythm and sequence. Here is a universal non-verbal language that speaks through the eloquence of shared symbol. Dance is an ancient sacred form. In ancient Egypt Hathor was the Goddess of music and dance. Her priestesses performed sacred dance to evoke the presence of divine beauty and harmony. The sacred dance was able to take participants and worshippers into states of ecstatic bliss. In India temple dancers portrayed the stories of the deities in movement and gesture. In Bali dance was offered in the temple. The great traditions of sacred dance have been eclipsed. We are left with the desire to reconnect, to revitalize and renew for the spirit of the dance never dies.

In the infancy of the twentieth century the free-spirited Isadora Duncan reinterpreted movement during a time of oppressive materialism and formality; her dancing was radical. She found inspiration in the classical past of Greece and danced barefoot in simple flowing garments. She expressed the liberation of the human spirit through spontaneous and graceful movement. She was unique; with her passing this exuberant but all too brief flirtation with dance of the spirit was over. Her life revitalized the sacred dance once again. She gave others the courage to share in the dance of life. As the twentieth century unfolded others again looked to the spiritual dimensions of dance. Rudolph Steiner, whose spiritual vision encompassed every aspect of the mundane life from organic farming to education, also saw the spiritual in dance. He created a new approach to

movement, which he called Eurythmy. This combined movement
and gesture in synchronous harmony with the spoken word.
Accordingly every consonant corresponds to a movement. The
movements of Eurythmy are soft and flowing, gentle and
expressive. He wrote, 'Man is a form proceeding out of
movement. Eurythmy is a continuation of divine movement, of
the divine form in man. By means of Eurythmy man approaches
nearer to the divine.'

More recently still there has been a revival of circle dancing as
spiritual expression. The circle is a natural symbol. The circular
dance easily becomes the cycle of the year, the girdle of the
zodiac, or simply the gathering of the clan. As we dance in the
circle, we also tread the magic circle and create a shared sacred
space. As the circle naturally expresses human interaction and
understanding, so spinning or whirling also seems to be a
natural movement. Children often spin and whirl in playground
games until giddiness and laughter take over. Since the earth
spins on its axis, spinning too is a symbolic movement. The Sufi
Master Jaluddin Rumi founded the Mevlevi Order which is
more commonly known as the Order of Whirling Dervishes.
The whirling dance is a moving meditation. The dancer
undertakes a series of inner images which bind the cosmic to the
mundane, the individual to creation. The dance expresses the
unity of life, through the unity of thought and action. The right
hand of the dancer is upturned to receive divine blessing. The
left hand points down to transmit the living presence to the
world. Curiously, this dance has been banned, though now
special permits are given to perform it for tourists; the sacred is
secularized and put up for sale.

The teacher Osho writes that, 'Whirling is one of the most
ancient techniques, one of the most forceful. It is so deep that
even a single experience can make you totally different.'[5] He
gives practical suggestions for attempting to whirl. The best
teacher is probably experience, however. Following Osho's
instructions, select dynamic music to rouse the spirit and carry
you into whirling. Start with hands crossed on the shoulders and
remember to return to this position if you feel dizzy. Begin to
rotate on your left foot by using the right foot to drive the body
around. Your left foot is like an anchor to the ground. The
whirling is done on the spot in an anti-clockwise direction. The
right arm is held high, palm upwards and the left arm is held
low, palm downwards. Keep the eyes open but unfocused so
that images become blurred and flowing. Although Osho

suggests rotating slowly for the first 15 minutes before building up speed, it is quite likely that you will find this an ambitious goal. Just start and see how whirling feels for you. If you do manage to build up to speed, you will find it difficult to remain upright. When this happens your body will fall by itself. Just let yourself fall. If you have been whirling for an hour then slow down gradually taking 10 minutes or more. Once you have fallen, move into the second part of the meditation, which is to roll onto your front and feel yourself blending into the earth. Rest and remain inactive for at least 15 minutes. The free dance of Isadora Duncan, the dance language of Rudolph Steiner and the whirling meditation of Rumi are all expressions of our ability to unite the spiritual with the material and harmonize mind, body and spirit through all-pervading consciousness, which is the way of activity.

Don't be restricted by definitions, it is impossible to restrict movement or music. Just dance.

The allegorical garden

It is a spot beyond imagination
Delighted to the heart, where roses bloom,
And sparkling fountains murmur – where the earth
Is rich with many-coloured flowers; and musk
Floats on the gentle breezes, hyacinths
And lilies add their perfume – golden fruits
Weigh down the branches of the lofty trees.

Firdawsi

What does your garden mean to you? Is it a place of delight or a place of drudgery? Is it heaven on earth or hell on earth? Whatever your garden is for you, to the Persians the garden represented an image of paradise. It provided the physical opportunity to create an image of the celestial. The gardens of Paradise are described in the Qur'an (55: 45–75). The four gardens within the Paradise Garden are the Garden of the Soul, the Garden of the Heart, the Garden of the Spirit and the Garden of the Essence. These are the four stages through which the mystic travels. This description has inspired a long lived and beautiful tradition of the garden as spiritual allegory. Here is a way of activity that literally combines the spiritual and the earthly. For as virgin soil is landscaped it is redesigned in the image of the divine through proportion, arrangement metaphor and living symbol.

Water was a constant theme in the form of pools, lakes, channels and fountains. More than merely forming a beautiful sight in the garden, water represented the spiritual light. As a fountain the spiritual light nourished and fed the whole garden. It imparted a full flavour to the many fruits. Plums, cherries, quinces, lemons, apricots, mulberries, figs, oranges, limes, pomegranates and grapes were a luscious harvest, but such fruits also represented thoughts nurtured on the Tree of Life. Water was admired at its surface for its reflective sheen as a mirror of passing reality. The surface was at times decorated with strewn rose petals or beautified by lilies in bloom. Open water channels were lined with blue tiles to deepen the reception of colour and the sound of splashing water was enhanced by changes of level to awaken perception. Every detail was important in this living symbolic landscape. The depths of the larger pools symbolized the dark and unfathomable mystery of life itself. The Persian garden was lit by many flowers but most favoured was the rose. This was already rich with symbolic and mystical connotation from spiritual poetry where the beloved, the soul, was identified with the rose. Trees were planted in abundance as symbols of life and immortality.

Here is an activity that you can make your own. Symbolic planting and colour can be brought to life in the simplest garden. Spiritual ideas and themes can be represented in ways of your own choosing. Let your creativity and spiritual inspiration live. The garden lives too. Here is a place for both contemplative meditation and active meditation. Here is where you can meet Gaia through the round of the seasons. If you love the engagement of the gardening process from seed to plant, you have many opportunities to interact with the living energies of nature. Here is a way of participation – be inventive, be creative. The garden lives, it reveals the interdependence of all things. Let head, heart and hands be united through a single expression and join the way of activity.

Sacred shrines

> The act of creating sacred space recapitulates the stages of creation.
>
> Patee Kryder, *Sacred Ground to Sacred Space*

As meditation creates changes in consciousness, so aspirations, goals and intentions change too. We become more discriminating and more focused on what is important to us. As this process gathers momentum, it becomes quite natural to represent these areas through symbol and image. We join the ancient and universal tradition of shrinemakers and keepers. Here too is a way of activity as we select items of importance and colours of significance to express our spiritual presence. Shrine building begins with a simple question: what is sacred to you? Answering the question not in words but representations takes us towards the building of a personal shrine. This can be very simple. It need be no more than a small space on a shelf or table top. It does not even need to draw attention to itself; an arrangement of flowers, stones or shells with a small candle is as eloquent as anything large and ornate. The shrine merely represents the fact that you choose outwardly to recognize what you inwardly acknowledge to be sacred. The items will change as you change.

The family shrine or household shrine is very common in the East but rather uncommon in the West where state-based religion and communal worship has dominated. Creating a shrine as a focal point for your spiritual life is a creative affirmation of your spiritual intent. Shrine building will put you in touch with the great artistic and cultural traditions of the world for which civilization has not built shrines. If you follow this impetus, you will encounter archetypal forms in numerous historical guises. You will discover the inner significance of geometry, sacred architecture and colour. You will find the sacred symbols of peoples past and present but most of all you will find what is sacred to you. Here is the place for the beautiful and the natural, the painted and the crafted, the constructed and the found. Here is the place for the sacred in your home and heart.

The difference between thinking and doing is substantial. The mind creates rapidly and without limitation. Images can be conjured from the imagination or from memory. Mental images enjoy no permanent form and remain invisible to all but the creator. When a vision is translated into physical form it becomes tangible and accessible. The shrine encapsulates feeling and intent, aspiration and devotion, which transcend the purely intellectual mind. Sacred images serve as a focus for further meditation, which gives rise to new insight and inspiration in a dynamic and continuous relationship.

If there is one thing we should recognize in the variety of spiritual expressions, it is simply that such avenues are without number. The depth and breadth of the original Egyptian vision shows us that every avenue in life can be made sacred. Medicine and astronomy, mathematics and dance, geometry and architecture, ceremony and art, all take the inner meditative world into the physical realm where vision is made reality, inspiration is made concrete, hope is made tangible. This is the challenge. Find your own expression in the world. Create your own way of action. Draw upon the past. Redefine it in the present and let it create the future.

08

changing: the flow of life

In this chapter you will learn:
- the natural rhythms of time
- to understand impermanence.

Time and tide

The fabric of our ordinary lives appears so regular, so predictable, sometimes even stagnant. It is easy to see the life of home and work, commitment and responsibility as a permanent fixture. This is always illusory. Within routine, change is constant. Nothing is permanent; this is the flow of life. It is the Demon Impermanence who holds the Wheel of Life in his clutches; he has us all in his grip, whether we know it or not. Recognizing the impermanence of all things is a powerful realization. The news of a life-threatening illness can shake us to the core; it brings us face to face with our own impermanence. So often such news serves to galvanize intentions and focus motivations. Priorities shift instantly and we suddenly see what is really important with devastating clarity. Such shocks put life in perspective. But it need not take a tragedy to remind us of the obvious. We can keep our priorities in focus through choice and awareness. We cannot hide in the delusion of permanence. We cannot halt the passing of time. We cannot control the flow of life, but we can flow with it.

Contemporary Western society is organized by the clock and the timetable, the meeting and the schedule, the diary and the planner. Being on time is a virtue, being late is unforgivable. This continual deference to the clock is highly stressful and places daily life within shared constraints. While it seems impossible to escape the obligations of timekeeping in the outer world, we might benefit by keeping this in balance with an inner sense of time. Yet Nature has her own rhythms too. Sunrise and sunset are the twin poles of the natural day. There is something wonderfully magical as the sun appears over the horizon and the day breaks. The moment of sunset is equally wonderful as the sun sinks and darkness spreads. These are Nature's markers, the continual play of change and interdependency. Have you watched the sun rise? Have you watched the sun set?

Sunrise and sunset have a reality which transcends the clock and the timekeeping devices of our own world. As we watch the moment of sunrise, we can reflect upon the countless generations who have done the same. As we watch daybreak we can know that civilizations now long dead also observed the same event. Who has not seen the sun rise and set? Peoples unknown and unnamed, peoples forgotten in memory and distant in time have lived by the moments of dawn and dusk. The sun opens and closes for all: Buddhists and Hindus, Sikhs and Sufis, Christians and Muslims alike. Watching the coming and going of day and night puts us in touch with the flow of life which is change. Take sunrise and sunset as your meditations and let nature be your teacher.

The sun has much to teach the observant watcher for it marks out seasonal rhythms too. The place of sunrise and sunset on the horizon move as the year progresses. This apparently moving light traces out a seasonal dance. We no longer live upon the empty horizon; we have forgotten the dance of the sun. Midsummer and midwinter are the twin poles of the solar year, so why not make the effort to become conscious of this fundamental pattern. The sun on the horizon keeps us in touch with the flow of life. These seasonal solstice landmarks hold the cycle of the year. These are the natural cycles, which cannot be denied, moved or mistaken. The cycle of the natural year has become swamped by the demands we place on ourselves. Less technological societies have taken these seasonal landmarks as the basis for spiritual celebration and festivity. As the wheel of the year turns, so we turn too. As we internalize this natural movement, we begin to realize that all is moving, the earth turns constantly on its own axis and also takes up its own orbit through space. The moon dances around the earth too. Nothing is still. The cosmic dance is an ancient image for the interplay of creation and we forget the dance only at our own cost.

When we replace the cosmic dance with a frozen, hard-edged reality, we compartmentalize life into things separated by insurmountable boundaries. We may not realize it but we have already taken a step towards freezing the movement of the life we live. Realizing the interdependence of all existence prevents us from committing this fatal flaw. We see interdependence in every way in every day, though we often remain unconscious of it. We see it at every level of life from the cosmic to the mundane. It is demonstrated for us continuously and totally. All we need to do is become aware of this great interdependent web that holds us all. The phenomena that define the shape of our lives are all interdependent pieces of a vast jigsaw of being, day and night, sunrise and sunset, solstice and equinox. Dawn and dusk, sunlight and moonlight each exist in relationship, not as separate objects. The relationship between sun and moon shows us an interdependent relationship that we so often take for granted. The moon has no light of its own but reflects the light of the sun to us, which we see in a cyclic pattern of light and dark. The moon is full when it is opposite the light of the sun and it is dark when it receives no light from the sun. Its growing and diminishing, the waxing and waning of the moon, are statements of relationship. The lunar cycle of 29½ days is a statement of interdependence. Watch the Moon and take interdependence as your theme; once you have begun to see the interdependence of all life, you will understand that this is the web that supports your existence and you will move a step closer to the flow of life.

EXERCISE 8.1 INTERDEPENDENCE

This is an active meditation that involves you more deeply in the rhythms of the natural world. Take the movement of the moon as your theme. Observe it when you can, although this will depend on the prevailing conditions. Observe its changing light and shape as manifestations of interdependence between the movements of earth and moon in relation to the sun. This brings a wonderful sense of the cosmos into your life.

Let us also take up the invitation extended by Thich Nhat Hanh:

> I invite you to meditate with me. Please sit in a position that you find relaxing, so that you are comfortable, and place your attention on your breathing, letting it become gentle, very light. After a few moments, move your attention to the feelings in your body. If you feel any pain or discomfort, or if you feel anything pleasurable, bring your attention there and enjoy the feeling with all of your awakened consciousness. After a little while, notice the functions of your different organs – your heart, lungs, kidneys, digestive system and so forth. Notice the blood flowing like a river through the countryside, nourishing the fields with fresh water. You know that this river of blood nourishes all the cells of your body and that your organs composed of cells enrich, purify and propel the blood. All the body's organs, including the nervous system and glands, rely on each other for existence. Every organ implies the existence of all other things. This is called 'the interdependence of all things'.[1]

The body is a wonderful expression of interdependence, so let us acknowledge it in consciousness. When you have become conscious of interdependence, you become part of the interdependence and you step consciously into the dance to take up your rightful place in the great flow of life.

Flowing with daily life

Each thought, each action in the sunlight of awareness becomes sacred. In this light, no boundaries exist between the sacred and the profane.

Thich Nhat Hanh, *The Sun My Heart*

Once again we are indebted to the simple wisdom of Thich Nhat Hanh for the endearing book *Present Moment, Wonderful Moment*. His philosophy is so straightforward: if you live fully in every moment, you will live fully. Who can find fault with this. Meditation takes place from the foundations of everyday life. It develops and flowers within everyday life. Meditation is intimately and wholly related to everyday life and in turn everyday life is changed through meditation. For a moment stand back from the requirements of your everyday life – look at it with a detached eye. How do you go about the daily round? Do you engage with daily life or do you want every day to be over as quickly as possible? Does your daily life appear to be dull and monotonous? Are you awake in life or do you sleepwalk from one day to the next? Thich Nhat Hanh asks us, 'How many days slip by in forgetfulness? What are you doing with your life?'

Lama Govinda also addresses the way in which we perceive daily life: 'Habit kills intuition, because habit prevents living experience, direct perception.' [2] What have you done today? Where have you been today? What will you do tomorrow? Is your life governed by routine, habit and predictability? Don't be afraid to admit that it is, because routine, regularity and predictability form a big and important part of life. It is not regularity of lifestyle, but habitual thinking that destroys. Monastic life is orderly and disciplined. Paradoxically, it is the life of habit that gives freedom. What did you notice today? What did you notice about today or did it appear just like any other day to you? Does every day appear to be the same? Even a moment's clear reflection will show you that every day cannot be the same as another. What did you notice on your way to work? What were you aware of at work today? What did you notice at home today? Tomorrow, be conscious of the opportunity, become aware and you will find something new in tomorrow. Take meditation into your ordinary daily life. Take it with you when you walk or shop or visit a friend. Meditation is not confined to sitting in a meditation posture. It may begin in this way but it will in time expand into ordinary life. It becomes a way of looking at life, a way of seeing with open eyes. When your eyes are open, you will walk in the flow of life and be responsive to it.

Being here and now

> When I eat, I eat; when I sleep, I sleep.
> Traditional Zen saying

The simple words of Thich Naht Hanh take us back to the immediacy of every moment:

> If I am incapable of washing dishes joyfully, if I want to finish them quickly so I can go and have a cup of tea, I will be equally incapable of drinking the tea joyfully. With the cup in my hands I will be thinking about what to do next, and the fragrance and the flavour of the tea together with the pleasure of drinking it will be lost. I will always be dragged into the future, never able to live in the present moment.[3]

Our lives may be very different, yet we may still benefit from the application of such a simple philosophy. How often do our minds stray from the present to the future where plans lie waiting for us or to the past where we replay conversations and encounters in our minds over and over again. Thich Naht Hanh is not unaware of the predicament of the Western lifestyle: 'You may ask how can you nourish awareness while washing dishes, binding books, or working in a factory or an office. I think you have to find your own answer.'[4] He gently reminds us of mindful living: 'Do whatever you can to keep the light of awareness shining inside yourself.' The problem obviously pre-dates the present for there is a classic Zen story that makes the same point. A disciple asks the master, 'Master, how do you put enlightenment into action? How do you practise it in everyday life?' 'By eating and by sleeping', replied the master. 'But master, everybody sleeps and everybody eats.' 'But not everybody eats when they eat and not everybody sleeps when they sleep.' Thich Nhat Hanh lives out the truth of the tale: 'I learned to maintain awareness during all activities – weeding the garden, raking leaves around the pond, washing the dishes in the kitchen.'[5] In the same vein Rabbi Nachman observed: 'Man's world consists of nothing except the day and the hour that he stands in now. Tomorrow is a completely different world.' He also remarked 'yesterday and tomorrow do not exist'.[6] The message is the same no matter which source it comes from. The meaning is clear regardless of the words that convey it to us. Be awake to life at every moment. What a simple straightforward message this really is. Yet how we long to hear a complicated philosophy and how we yearn to know a great secret. How can anything so important turn out to be so simple!

EXERCISE 8.2 THE PRESENT MOMENT

In your ordinary and everyday life, just be focused in the present moment. This is such a simple idea which is hard to carry out as we evade the moment and retreat into the imagined future or sentimental past. Observe yourself over a short period and see how quickly your mind tries to escape, then bring yourself back to the present moment.

So much of life is bound up with relationships, family and friends. Few are the folk who choose to give up this base in favour of the monastic life. Family life with all its normal ups and downs is the place where mindfulness can serve us well. Running a home and bringing up a family is continually demanding. Mindfulness is ever required in relationships if we are to interact with sensitivity and understanding. It could be argued that it is within family life and ordinary circumstances that mindfulness practice is tested to capacity. How many busy mothers would not cheerfully choose a monastic retreat – just briefly of course – perhaps until the regular ritual of children's bedtime has passed anyway! In many ways mindfulness is an extension of the loving care given by parents in the normal course of life. Christine Feldman, mother of two and co-founder of a meditation retreat centre in Devon, affirms what every parent knows: 'Parenting challenges you at every level of your being. All the things that are important in meditation practice – patience, forgiveness, letting go, compassion, steadfastness and equanimity – are the things that are also important in parenting. Children provide opportunities to develop, nurture and nourish these qualities in direct and dynamic ways.'[7] A parent seeks to be aware of a child's needs, even the unspoken ones, to listen to what is said both in word and intent, to understand developmental needs and to be responsive and loving. If such needs were mindlessly ignored, only unhappiness would follow. So mindfulness does not have to be treated as an esoteric or arcane discipline; you are already mindful.

Jon Kabat-Zinn is a doctor who writes in an easy style about Buddhism and its place in contemporary American life. He brings Buddhist principle right into the home where it belongs. He suggests:

> Try to use ordinary, repetitive occasions in your own house as invitations to practise mindfulness. Going to the front door, answering the telephone, seeking out someone else in the house to speak with, going to the bathroom, getting the laundry out of the dryer, going to the refrigerator can all be occasions to slow down and be more in touch with each present moment.[8]

Why not take his advice, simple as it is. Bring mindful meditation into the front room and the kitchen, indeed bring it into the whole house.

Taking mindfulness into everyday life begins the process of living transformation. Daily mindfulness brings gains in simple straightforward awareness, but beyond this daily mindfulness serves a deeper purpose. Our psychological health is much bound up with the way in which we deal with the ordinary situations, circumstances and relationships of life. If we store the hurt, whether real or imaginary, from every encounter with friend or foe, ally or enemy, we accrue much personal baggage in the form of painful memories, hidden resentments, secret fears or repressed anger. All these settle like lead weights in the depths of our being and prevent us from being open to the flow of life, so we cannot be open. We are too busy defending and protecting ourselves from being wounded in the same way again. Mindfulness enables us to view all interactions with a clear but detached eye; we can understand the inner dynamics of every situation, no matter how simple. We can see resentments as they arise, recognize old wounds and potential trigger points. Mindful awareness acts as a self-clearing process in the present moment. We cannot undo the past and the baggage already accrued, but we do not have to pick up any more emotional baggage. Lama Govinda rightly says:

> If we allow the past undissolved and undigested to sink into the subconscious, the past becomes the germ of uncontrollable – because unconscious – drives and impulses. Only those things which we have perfectly

understood and consciously penetrated can be mastered and can have no more power over us. The methods of healing employed by modern psychotherapy as well as by most ancient meditation practices are based on this principle.[9]

Here is a simple example of this principle in practice. It is taken from Jon Kabat-Zinn's book *Mindfulness Meditation for Everyday Life*:

Cat food lessons

I hate finding caked cat dishes in the kitchen sink along with ours, I'm not sure why this pushes my buttons so strongly, but it does. First I get angry. Then the anger gets more personal and I find myself directing it at whoever I think is the culprit, which is usually my wife. I feel hurt because she doesn't respect my feelings. I tell her on countless occasions that I don't like it, that it disgusts me. I've asked her as politely as I know how not to do it but she often does it anyway. She feels I'm being silly and compulsive, and when she's pressed for time, she leaves the caked cat dishes soaking in the sink. Recently I've noticed that I'm not getting so bent out of shape about this.

I observe the anger as it starts rising in me. It turns out that it is preceded by a mild feeling of revulsion. Then I notice the stirring of a feeling of betrayal which is not so mild. I have taken to experimenting with my reactions at the kitchen sink by watching them very closely without acting on them. I can report that the initial feeling of revulsion is not at all that bad if I stay with it, and breathe with it, and permit myself just to feel it, it actually goes away in a second or two. I have also noticed that it is the sense of betrayal, of being thwarted in my wishes, that makes me much more mad than the cat food itself. So I discover, it's not really the cat food by itself that is the source of my anger. Then I remember my wife and my kids and see the whole thing differently. They think I am making a big deal out of nothing, and that while they will try to respect my wishes when it feels reasonable to them, at other times it doesn't and they just do it anyway, maybe without thinking about me at all. So I have stopped taking it personally. When I really don't want cat food in the sink, I roll up my sleeves and I clean the dishes in that moment. Otherwise I just leave them there and go away. We no longer have fights about it. In fact I find myself smiling now when I do come across the offending objects in the sink. After all they have taught me a lot.[10]

This honest and simple anecdote shows mindfulness in daily life in the nitty-gritty of family dynamics. Here is the flow of ordinary life in domestic circumstances. Awareness brings its own resolution. If meditation practice is ultimately concerned with the realization of the full human being, then daily life in whatever form it takes serves as the seedbed where we can slowly and organically grow into ourselves. When we see life as an open experience, we can see ourselves as constantly becoming. When we view life as a closed loop, we simply cease to grow. We close the doors to the future and we close ourselves to change and new experience. Daily life is the place where we can plant the seeds of the person we want to become.

Spiritual aspiration is often symbolized by an arrow in flight. The arrow is loosed into the future, it lands like a marker for us. Reflect on those qualities that will support your future practice and those qualities that will not. To clarify your ideas make a list. It is likely that qualities such as patience, kindness, simplicity, trust and forgiveness will be among your list of supporting qualities. On the other hand anger, fear, intolerance, laziness and impatience will probably be on your list of non-supportive qualities. Spend some time making your list. When it is complete look at yourself and honestly evaluate the way in which these qualities function within you. Decide which qualities you need to develop and which need to be diminished. When you have come to a decision be prepared to use daily life as the opportunity to create change. Daily life presents us with continuous choices; to be kind or unkind, thoughtful or thoughtless, patient or impatient. Observe yourself. Particular situations probably create the same reactions over and over. As soon as we see the pattern, we are in a position to intervene and consciously react differently. This kind of self-observation is not unique to Buddhism. Rabbi Nachman, a founder of the Hasidic movement, stressed the importance of taking stock regularly: 'You must therefore make sure to set aside a specific time each day to calmly review your life.'[11]

EXERCISE 8.3 CULTIVATING QUALITIES

Using the list of qualities you have chosen, select one attribute. Take this as a theme for your meditation. Reflect on it as a quality in the abstract and also try to understand how this quality operates in your life currently. In your own mind affirm how you would like this quality to function, perhaps more strongly, perhaps less obviously. Affirm what you want; see the benefits for yourself and those closely involved in your life too. A new quality cannot come to birth overnight, so plant the seed gently within yourself and nurture it well. As for any quality you might wish to leave behind, don't try to kill it at a stroke. It has served you well so why not say thank you for its presence in your life. This will make the transition more gentle. Meditation and life merge. The seamless garment of being and becoming emerges.

Impermanence: the teacher

> You don't know know what you've got till it's gone.
> Joni Mitchell

The words of the song ring horribly true for all of us. How many times have we wished to put the clock back or to be given a second chance? But time moves on relentlessly and second chances are few and far between. How often do we regret the things said or unsaid, the unfinished business, the unresolved issues that we leave in our wake? Buddhists believe that here lies the fuel of our future karma. Here are seeds waiting to come to fruition in the future. Whether we believe in the power of unfinished business to draw us back into future incarnations or not, we can still recognize unfinished business in ourselves. It is easy to live in pretence. It often seems preferable to truth. The truth is that human life is limited and we have an impermanent form in an ever changing world. Change and impermanence are frightening for we most often seek security and stability. When we only remember security and forget impermanence, we have missed the fundamental paradox of being alive. When we remember paradox, we look towards truth. Impermanence is the last thing we wish to face.

How reticent we are to talk about death, the last taboo. How reticent we are even to think about death. Death remains the greatest fear of all. Our fear is not diminished by ignoring this reality. Who feels comfortable thinking about their own death?

Who is willing to take personal death as a subject for meditation. Yet besides birth, death is perhaps the only other certainty. And yet this is our greatest fear. It holds the terror of the unknown and the call of the inevitable. Rather than face this certain destiny, we choose to ignore this reality until the very moment when death comes calling. Until we face death, we are not free to find life. Spiritual traditions universally offer meditations on death. The Sufis say, 'die before you die'. Osho's words too have an immediacy:

> Start meditating on death. And whenever you feel death close by, go into it through the door of love, through the door of meditation, through the door of a man dying. And if some day you are dying – and the day is going to come one day – receive it in joy, benediction. And if you can receive death in joy and benediction, you will attain to the greatest peak, because death is the crescendo of life.[12]

Osho died on 19 January 1990.

If we seek life, we too must face the reality of death as all the previous generations of spiritual travellers have done. Our fears will not be unique and our worries will not be personal, but a restatement of all the human fears and concerns down the ages. Buddhism asks that we address the subject of death. It offers graduated meditations that bring us face to face with the concept of death through small steps. The first step is to reflect that death is inevitable. We need to think about the fact that everybody is going to die and that there is no place we can go to avoid death. Second, we are asked to reflect on the fact that the time of death is uncertain. We do not have a fixed lifespan. We do not know when death will come. Small things can cause our death and there is no guarantee of a long life. Third, we are asked to envisage the close of life and ponder upon what has been worthwhile. These three stages help us find what is really important in our lives.

There have been many religious concepts about the significance of death. These are divided into two main schools of thought. The first proposes a linear model that maintains that one physical life is a preparation for the greater life, which takes place in another state beyond death. We can recognize this view in Christianity for example. The second view suggests a cyclic model of becoming through reincarnation. The cyclic model and the linear model are undoubtedly at odds with each other in many ways. The idea of many lives is powerfully suggestive of continuous becoming. The idea of a single physical life suggests becoming only with a framework of closure. The template we choose shapes the way we live our life, the beliefs we seek out and the manner of our dying. It is curious that both models, which seem so different, have resulted in the same tendency, which is to deny the importance of life in this world.

Perhaps a new model shall come into being. If we love life, let us affirm life. If we take the wheel as our model, let us affirm that life on the wheel is good. Why seek nirvana when nirvana and samasara are one? Let us choose life. If we live in the moment, death will have no fear. If the one-life model is your guiding light, affirm it fully and live it here and now. Heaven can wait. It is the certainty of death that provides life with its meaning, so, in our quest for meaning, let us also face the reality of death.

09

openness: the illumined mind

In this chapter you will learn:
- about the *koan*
- about the Nine Stages of Mental Quiescence
- about the seven stages of wisdom.

When man sits,
then the coarse passions subside
and the luminous mind
arises in awareness:
Thus consciousness is illuminated.

Meister Eckhart

The light of consciousness

The search for consciousness remains as tantalizing as ever. Both East and West approach the same territory from different perspectives. The West takes empirical research as its standard and seeks to study consciousness from the outside. The East explores consciousness from within by acting directly upon it. In the West we are without an accepted metaphysical framework. Such models belong only to the mystical and have not crossed the boundary into mainstream science. We too are driven by the quest to discover mind, yet we continue to search for it almost exclusively by looking into the brain and its workings. Experiment and research are still the favoured tools for enquiring into consciousness. We are convinced that scientific objectivity is our safeguard. Yet the scientific method is only another projection of consciousness. Only consciousness can investigate consciousness, even when it is dressed up as empirical research.

Eastern spirituality presents a quite different paradigm. Consciousness has been investigated through the long centuries of observation, interaction and participation. Using an Eastern model, consciousness is described by the term *citta*. The verb cit means to perceive, to notice, to know, to understand, to long for, to desire and to remind. As a noun *cit* means emotion, intellect, feeling, disposition, vision, heart, soul and Brahman. Consciousness can be nurtured through cultivation, observation, progressive refinement and the development of detachment and renunciation. *Cinta* refers to disturbed or anxious thoughts and *cintana* means deliberate thinking; both are facets of *citta*. Consciousness is described by its actions. It is not reduced to an object that we will one day find like a needle in a cosmic haystack. When we notice, perceive, know, understand, long for, desire and even remind ourselves, we employ consciousness. When we feel emotion or use the intellect, a consciousness is at work. When we are moved by vision or heart, then *citta* is active within us. When we seek soul and the divine, *citta* is awake. When we know that we are a part of the whole, we have realized **bodhicitta**. When we actively seek to cultivate *citta*, we undertake the progressive refinement of this consciousness through the development of observation and detachment. Here is a definition that is rich with possibility and meaning for our life. Here is a definition that places consciousness directly in human affairs, not the laboratory. Moreover *citta*, the seat of intelligence, is the individual counterpart of **mahat,** the universal consciousness. In the temples of India it is common to find an image of stone and a second and related bronze image. The bronze image is carried out in procession. It represents the personal or individual self. The stone image is permanently fixed and represents the universality of the soul. Western science has nothing to say about universal consciousness. The East, however, has much to say about it.

Koans: puzzles without solutions

> Westerners seem to have particular difficulty in learning to let go of reason, will and memory, in order to find absolute stillness.
> Hugo M. Enomiya-Lassalle, *The Practice of Zen Meditation*

When we are ready to come to grips with fundamental questions, it does not take much thought to discover that we cannot answer the very questions that trouble us. In fact the harder we think, the more confused we become. Spiritual systems invariably shift the focus of the quest away from the intellect to the development of insight and wisdom. Zen takes an even more radical stand. Zen has no time for philosophical speculation or metaphysical doctrine. Its teaching moments are not designed to fill the mind with concepts or cosmological models, but to put the student into a direct relationship with the Buddha nature, absolute truth. Since the intellect is considered to be inadequate to the task, it should be completely bypassed. As the hold of the intellect is so great, it has to be broken at a stroke; there can be no compromise with sweet reason. The mind breaker is the *koan*, which is the unique contribution of Zen.

The *koan* presents the student with a conundrum: since it is a riddle of sorts it cannot be solved through logic or reason. It demands something more from the student – it demands a breakthrough into a new consciousness. The *koan* leads the pupil into an impasse from which there is no escape. There is neither detour into the symbolic nor recourse to logic. There is only the mind breaker and the student. Most *koans* are the recorded sayings of early Zen Masters. For instance, a monk once asked Master Joshu, 'Has a dog a Buddha nature or not?' Joshu gave the now famous reply, 'Mu'. The Zen Master Hakuin one day clapped his hands, then silently raised one and asked, 'What is the sound of one hand clapping?' Thus another *koan* was born.

Imagine yourself in the place of the pupil: 'What is the sound of one hand clapping?'! We immediately sense the conundrum. We hear the words and we feel a frisson of excitement arising in the mind. We know that the question calls for an answer, but how can we answer this puzzle without solution? Working with a *koan* is constant. The first attempts to wrestle it to the ground through the intellect are soon abandoned. How else can understanding be achieved without resource to the reasoning mind. Here is the paradox that grips the student. It creates an intense inner dilemma. Zen is not concerned with mind as normally understood, but in reaching a state described as No-mind, which is the true nature where thinking stops. The *koan* is held in the mind by day and night. The *koan* fills consciousness until consciousness becomes emptied in the struggle. Even at this point there is no escape because the mind breaker is at work. Continuous practice can precipitate a breakthrough. In the tradition of the teacher–pupil relationship, the student will be summoned to the daily interview called the **dokusan** where the student is asked to demonstrate an understanding of the *koan*. This is not an opportunity for intellectual analysis. The Zen Master, the Roshi, assesses the understanding of the student through gesture, voice, tone, presence, quality of movement, expression and other signs that indicate the depth and penetration of the *koan*. Perhaps the student will be sent back for further work, or perhaps the student's breakthrough will be accepted.

Certain *koans* have passed from the monastery precincts into the outer world. Our familiarity with a mere handful of *koans* has tended to eclipse the fact that the tradition holds many more that have never reached Western shores. *The Mumonkan* is a collection of 48 *koans*, which was compiled by the Zen Master, Mumon. The work includes a commentary to assist the student: every assistance is given to aid the student in the interior struggle. It remains customary for a Zen master to deliver a commentary upon the *koan*. However, once again paradox prevails, as the commentary is no commentary. The teisho is not a lecture or a sermon, but it is an offering to the Buddha that is delivered with ceremonial solemnity. The book of *koans* is carried in by an attendant and all those present bow their heads as a sign of humility as the Roshi proceeds to the altar. Then all those present offer three prostrations to the altar, led by the Roshi, to show gratitude, reverence and humility towards the Buddha and the Patriarchs of the tradition. The *teisho* is given daily and often twice daily. The Roshi faces the altar, not the gathering. There is no note-taking and there is nothing but focused awareness. The ceremonial setting directs the mind away from any attempt to remain in an intellectual mode of reception. There are no questions, there is no attempt to explain the meaning of the *koan*; there is only the encounter with the *koan*. The commentary on 'Mu' provides a brief insight into the nature of the traditional style:

> Then concentrate on this 'Mu' with your 360 bones and the 84,000 pores and transform your whole body into one big search. Work diligently on it day and night. Do not attempt any nihilistic or dualistic interpretations. It is as if you had gulped down a red hot ball and you cannot now spit it out. Completely discard your illusory, discriminating knowledge and your hitherto leaning and work still harder. After a while your efforts will bear fruit, distinctions (for example inside and outside) will become naturally one. You will be bewildered – like someone who has had a wonderful dream: one only knows it in oneself. Suddenly you will break through the barrier. You will startle heaven and shake the earth. How shall one strive for it? With all your might, work on this 'Mu' and become 'Mu'.[1]

These are the words of the classic commentary, which are brought to life in the daily *teisho*. We hear the words, but what we do not hear is the delivery of charged words, gestures and subtle placement of ideas, which makes every commentary unique and electrifying. The Roshi does not eulogize or sermonize but uniquely 'strikes against' the *koan* from the *hara* centre. The Zen student is likewise taught to focus the mind within this centre, which is located between the navel and the pelvis. Here in this extraordinary setting, through the vehicle of a conundrum, the master may facilitate a moment of cataclysmic breakthrough in the pupil as No-mind and No-mind meet not in the head but in the belly!

These rarefied practices of Zen may seem to be a million miles away from the hurly-burly of the everyday. The average person in the street has little time for such esoteric interchange. The demands of work and play are far more pressing. Ordinary life seems complicated enough. Yet the message behind Zen and all spiritual traditions remains directly applicable to the everyday. Everyday life as it is normally lived is the place of the great illusion. This concept is by itself worthy of considerable thought and contemplation. Here is a potentially shattering thought. Spend some time with this idea in your mind. What does it mean to you?

Making space in the mind

> The purpose of meditation is to awaken in us the sky-like nature of mind, and to introduce us to that which we really are, our unchanging pure awareness, which underlies the whole of life and death.
>
> Sogyal Rinpoche, *Meditation*

When the mind is illumined through awareness, self-consciousness can take root and grow steadily. The practice of direct awareness brings us to an increasingly deeper understanding of everything we do. This brings light into the darkened room of mixed motives, gut responses, inappropriate behaviour, confused actions, sporadic resolutions and laudable intentions, which mix and match to make up everyday life. With illumination comes the opportunity to reflect on choices, to consider outcomes, to weigh up actions and to consider effects. With illumination comes direct knowing, confident responses, clear direction and purposeful action. Who would willingly choose to dwell in the dark room of shifting shapes when the bright room of infinite space is only a conscious decision away?

Have you had the experience of the thoughts in your mind racing out of control and tumbling over each other like a racing cascade? Have you been kept awake at night by the mind working overtime with plans, anticipated outcomes, possible futures and wild imaginings? We have all experienced this, and the feelings that accompany such frenetic activity are not pleasant. We cannot rest, we do not sleep, and we rollercoaster through the emotions at breakneck speed and awake exhausted. We are tormented by our own thoughts, which we seem powerless to stop. Sogyal Rinpoche tells us that the work of meditation is to allow thoughts to slow down and this can only be a good thing. It is the antidote to the wild pace of unrestrained thought that robs us of mental peace.

Buddhism teaches that above and beyond the thinking process lies another level of mind. This is the True Mind. The deep ocean is not the wave briefly rippling across the surface. Similarly, the spaciousness of the True Mind is quite different from the continuous thought play that we know so well rippling through our minds. To begin to grasp the difference between the True Mind and the thinking mind, use the traditional Buddhist image for your meditation. Meditate on the image of a vast ocean. See waves rippling across the surface. The waves will never be still, since it is in the nature of the ocean to produce waves. But you can identify your mind with the great depths and the deep waters. The title Dalai Lama, which belongs to the highest office in Tibetan Buddhism, means Great Ocean. To become more aware of the greater mind we need to develop an awareness of the space beyond the stream of thoughts. This awareness is developed by watching the content of the mind from a detached perspective. Just sit quietly with eye-lids lowered, turn your attention inwards and merely observe what passes. Watch your own thoughts arising. Do this as if you were a detached observer. When thoughts arise just let them pass through the mind. Watching thoughts arise and fall, ebb and flow, provides a distance between the thought in consciousness and consciousness itself. This detached viewing begins to bring a sense of space in the mind. It is the beginning of mindfulness, it is the seed of insight.

Finding inner space by separating the mind from the thoughts of the mind is often a new and welcome discovery. Resting in this space is a welcome relief. Recognizing the different qualities of thought and space shows us a distinction between the temporary and the permanent, the ground of mind and the activity of mind. We can also learn when to think and when to rest.

EXERCISE 9.1 FINDING SPACE

You may find space in the mind in the following way. Sit in meditation and become aware of thoughts passing through. Watch these as a detached observer. Now search for the tiny moment between a thought passing and a thought appearing. Look for that moment and prolong it. Begin to enter the space between thoughts as they come and go. Rest in this space. Look for the difference between the mind and the thought, the ocean and the wave.

Sogyal Rinpoche suggests linking the breath to the moment of spaciousness:

> When you breathe out, just flow out with the outbreath. Each time you breathe out, you are letting go and releasing grasping. Imagine your breath dissolving in the all-pervading expanse of truth. Each time you breathe out and before you breathe in again, you will find that there is a natural gap, as the grasping dissolves. Rest in the gap in that open space and when, naturally you breathe in don't focus especially on the inbreath but go on resting your mind in the gap that has opened up.[2]

This is the way to openness and possibility. It is the opposite of the closed book, the set piece and the definitive statement. When we lose the capacity for openness we close the mind itself, and we deaden *citta* within us. Spaciousness is the open window through which the light of illumination can shine. The closed mind cannot acknowledge the possibility of illumination. The open mind is alive and the open mind can look and see. The open mind can receive the light of illumination.

The royal road

Meditation then is bringing the mind home.
Sogyal Rinpoche, *Meditation*

Meditation is often thought of as a journey of personal change. Though the idea has a contemporary ring it is not new. A traditional Tibetan series of images shows us the stages of the journey from inner chaos to calm, from mental confusion to clarity, from wild disorder to awareness. This is the royal road that takes us towards the place of inner illumination where true learning can flower. This particular journey is described as the Nine Stages of Mental Quiescence. Although this image is Tibetan it describes a universal process. In the sequence, the nature of mind is symbolized by an elephant. In the beginning the elephant is wild and untamed and it is a danger to life and limb. Training is required so that the beast can be of service to its owner. As the journey progresses, so the elephant changes colour from black to white. The colour black symbolizes the initial hindrances to attaining mental control. These are the distractions known in the Tibetan tradition as sinking and excitement. But we can think of them as being all the distractions and problems we find when we first set out to

figure 9.1 the Nine Stages of Mental Quiescence

concentrate on a given subject. We also see a monkey dancing wildly beside the path. The monkey symbolizes all the external distractions and excuses we give ourselves for not being steadfast in our meditation.

We also see five objects. These represent the distractions provided by the world of the senses. The mirror symbolizes the distractions of form. The cymbals represent the distractions of sound and the bowl of fruit represents the distractions of taste. The conch shell holding perfume represents the distractions of smell and finally the piece of cloth represents tactile sensation. We also see flames, which symbolize the energy and effort required at different stages of the journey. At the outset the flames are large but become smaller and finally are absent. The six curves of the path represent Listening, Reflection, Recollection, Alertness, Joyful Effort and Familiarity. It has been pointed out that the stages for establishing a waking consciousness are much like the stages that bring us to daily wakening, from the moment we hear the alarm to the familiarity with which we go through the morning routine.

The Nine Stages of Mental Quiescence

1 Initial fixation

In the first picture a man follows an elephant. He holds a goad, which is a sharp stick for urging on cattle that symbolizes alertness. This represents the first attempts to control the mind. The man is chasing after an elephant that is led by a monkey. Both the monkey and the elephant are coloured black. The man chases after his quarry waving the goad but he is too far away even to make contact. At this stage there is a lack of focus and external distractions are overwhelming. Great effort is required to focus on a given subject even briefly. The mind soon wanders again and it has to be returned to the subject through conscious effort. This stage is characterized by dullness of mind and mental fog, which often leads to sleep instead of meditation.

2 Increasing fixation

The man now carries a rope in addition to the goad. The rope represents the power of recollectedness. There has been some slight change in the representation of the elephant and the monkey. Small areas of white have started to appear on the previously all black creatures. However, the man has not yet caught the elephant. The flames are still large and the elephant remains wild.

3 Patch-like fixation

In this third phase, the man has now succeeded in roping the elephant. The elephant's head, which is now fully white, is turned towards the man and the elephant looks more peaceful. However, now the elephant carries a rabbit on its back. The rabbit symbolizes two particular kinds of distraction, mental sinking, gross and subtle. In other words some degree of concentration has been attained but it is still liable to disappear at the first opportunity.

4 Close fixation

At the fourth stage, alertness is now more important than recollection. Although the man holds the elephant by the rope, he is about to administer the goad. This means that the man is aware when concentration is flagging and is able to administer the corrective. The elephant is becoming increasingly white, indicating that transformation is taking place.

5 Invigoration

At the fifth stage, excitement has no power to distract. The mental quality of sinking has been brought under control. For the first time, the monkey falls behind the elephant. Most of the elephant is white now.

6 Pacification

Now for the first time, the man walks in front of the elephant and the monkey. He is leading the animals from the front and he exudes an air of authority. The elephant is now half-white and half-black and the flames surrounding the path are much reduced.

7 Complete pacification

The man now stands between the monkey and the elephant and both creatures seem obedient. The man has abandoned both rope and goad. Neither the monkey nor the elephant has much dark colouring left.

8 Single-pointedness

At this stage the monkey has disappeared. The elephant is totally white for the first time. The elephant follows the man and appears tamed.

9 Formal fixation

Finally, in the ninth stage, the elephant and man lie down together in complete harmony. The man is shown riding the elephant. The last picture shows the elephant and man together returning the way they have come. The man carries a torch and there are flames in the background that represent the newly established energy. We also see the man flying on the last curve of the path. Here is an image of release and liberation in contrast to the frantic activity at the start of the journey. These didactic images express the very real difficulties and frustrations common to all who attempt to catch and train the mind.

The six curves of the road represent the qualities of :

- *Listening*: How carefully do you listen? What do you choose to listen to?
- *Reflection*: On what do you reflect? What is the purpose of reflection?
- *Recollection*: Do you spend any time recollecting thoughts and ideas? Does a continuous thread run through your words, deeds and actions?
- *Alertness*: How alert are you at any given time of the day?
- *Joyful Effort*: Is your effort joyful or painful, willingly given or begrudged?
- *Familiarity*: Are you yet familiar with the landscape of the mind?

The light of insight

> Self examination is the key to insight, which is the key to wisdom.
>
> M. Scott-Peck, *Meditations from the Road*

Meditation may begin with concentration, but it does not end there. Concentration forms the launching pad, but insight forms the moment of take-off. Thinking and reflecting are only the beginning and lead to an intuitive state of consciousness in which the processes of thinking and reasoning come to an end and some kind of deeper vision takes over. The birth of insight is the crowning glory of the path, which begins with mindfulness. This is the Path of Insight, which is called **Vipassana** meditation. From the simple practice of mindfulness, insight, which is inner sight, will flower. Insight transcends the twin poles of the intellect and the imagination. It is neither the restricted logic of deduction nor the broad vision of inspiration, but a direct viewing into the nature of reality, no matter how brief. Insight is the eye of truth. It is a state of non-thinking, a moment of no-thought. It is a brief seeing, a fleeting and momentary enlightenment. This is a forerunner of fully blown revelation. Here is the place where creativity and originality can arise. Insight takes us into the reality, of a multi-dimensional consciousness. Who would willingly choose the flat hinterland of one-dimensional thinking when the vast expanses of a multi-dimensional consciousness are at hand? Insight begins to become operative in your mind when you suddenly know something with absolute certainty. It is the voice of intuition and the moment of realization. Insight takes us towards wisdom, the sustained viewing of things just as they are.

The light of wisdom

Wisdom is a living stream, not an icon to be preserved in a museum. Only when a practitioner finds the spring of wisdom in his or her own life can it flow to a future generation.

Thich Nhat Hanh, *The Sun My Heart*

We have found knowledge but failed to realize wisdom. Knowledge is much prized in Western culture. We have created plenty of it. We have knowledge of the stars and the deep oceans. We have knowledge of the minute world of microbiology and the invisible world of subatomic particles. We have knowledge of the minute and the massive, the body and the brain. Yet as a global community, over and over again, we fail to live together in peace. Knowledge, it seems, does not bring wisdom. The West has developed an extraordinary technology. We can reach the moon, perform keyhole surgery and monitor the baby in the womb. We build skyscrapers and underground transport systems. We have built the atomic bomb and now we are unravelling the genetic code. Yet wisdom eludes us.

The glamour of knowledge and the seductive power of technology so often lulls us deeper into a shared sleep. Knowledge brings its own problems and challenges. For example, scientists are now on the verge of cracking the genetic code, but this knowledge will doubtless confer a mixed blessing. The Pandora's box of knowledge can never be shut once it has been opened. We are so used to singing the praises of knowledge that it comes as a shock to hear another viewpoint. The words of Osho are direct and shattering: 'Knowledge is the curse, the calamity, the cancer. It is through knowledge that man becomes divided from the whole. Knowledge creates the distance.' He continues to dispose of the much treasured product of the human mind:

You see how knowledge creates distance, how knowledge becomes a barrier, how knowledge stands in between, how knowledge goes on increasing and the distances go on increasing, how innocence is lost through knowledge, how wonder is destroyed, crippled, murdered through knowledge, how life becomes a dull and boring affair, through knowledge. Mystery is lost and with mystery God is lost.

Osho's words as ever are delivered as a wake-up call. He strikes at knowledge, which is the life-blood of modern Western society. We are forced to consider where we stand in relation to knowledge. We are, in all probability, the recipients of a good education and we respect the many branches of knowledge that sustain the culture in which we live. Make no mistake, Osho does not seek to replace knowledge by ignorance, which is no spiritual virtue, but to render knowledge transparent through insight: 'Insight will burn your knowledge, and it will not be replaced by another knowledge.'[3] Do not seek knowledge, there is nothing to know. Do not burden yourself with theories. Every theory is but a construct. It is a second-hand guide to living reality. It will stand between you and your own realization. Have the confidence to know that you too can see directly. Look for the barrier that is preventing you from believing in your own innate power to find wisdom. Find the barrier in yourself, it is only made from words. Seek to dissolve the barrier that prevents you from believing that you have everything you need already. What is your answer to the question 'What is Wisdom?'? Patanjali offers seven states of wisdom to think about. Reflect on these suggestions as you wish. Use these thoughts as seeds for your own meditation. Have the courage to create your own list. Indulge in a moment's frivolity. Imagine if your list were to become the foundation for a tradition stretching for centuries into the future. When living realisations become crystallized, the moment of true seeing is handed on only as a freeze-dried fragment.

EXERCISE 9.2 HONOURING WISDOM

In your meditation, honour wisdom, however you perceive this.

The seven states of wisdom

1 Knowing that which has to be known.
2 Discarding that which has to be discarded.
3 Attaining that which has to be attained.
4 Doing that which has to be done.
5 Winning the goal that has to be won.

6 Freeing the intelligence from the pull of the **gunas** of nature.
7 Achieving emancipation of the soul so that it shines in its own light.

Additionally these states are further simplified as:

1 Understanding the body within and without.
2 Understanding energy and its uses.
3 Understanding mind.
4 Awareness of experience.
5 Awareness of pure quintessence, sentiment and beauty.
6 Understanding that an individual soul is a particle of the universal spirit.

As we move into a global age of shared communication, perhaps we will watch the marriage of Eastern wisdom and Western technology and find the union of spiritual truth and material value. Let us then, like the sages of all times and all traditions, look towards wisdom as our light on the horizon.

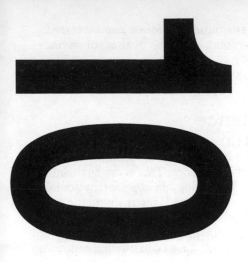

10

hearing: the power of sound

In this chapter you will learn:
- about the creative power of sound
- about mantra
- about the healing power of the voice.

The origin of healing by sound and music can be traced into prehistory and beyond, into the realms of myth, religion and the memory of the soul.

Olivia Dewhurst Maddock, *The Book of Sound Therapy*

The sound of silence

Television, radio, personal CD players and stereo systems, in-car sound systems, in-store music and wrap-around sound all contribute to a sound-filled experience. This is the environment we now take for granted. Technology brings instant sound to the home, the workplace and the car. This is mundane sound which is the voice of the world at work.

Where is silence now as you read these words? What sounds can you hear at this moment? Stop and become attuned to them. What do you hear? Where is silence for you? When did you last sit in silence? Perhaps the very word reminds you of the enforced silence in the library or the schoolroom. Yet silence need not be oppressive or uncomfortable. Silence is a powerful symbol for the qualities of emptiness and spaciousness, which we seek through meditation. The empty mind is the open mind; the spacious mind is the free mind. The silent moment is empty and spacious. Do you have any moments of silence in your life? Reflect for a moment upon the many different sounds that punctuate our lives: alarm calls, phone calls, radio and television in the home, piped music in shops, stereo sound in cars, traffic on the streets, machinery in the factory, technology in the office. Where is silence?

If we want silence we will need consciously to create it. How often do we turn on the radio or even the television 'just for company'? This is not conscious listening but unconscious listening. We fill the empty space with the noise of the human voice. We pay no attention to what is being said, we are simply happy with the sound of company. When an opportunity presents itself, you will be able to choose between sound and silence. What will you choose? Seek out a silent space, create a silent space and savour it. Silence teaches us how to value sound and sound teaches us how to value silence. It is no surprise to find that Henry Skolimowski, the advocate of ecological spirituality, values the spiritual silence: 'The triviality of our lives and the lack of space for reflection are closely connected. In our continuous rushing we lose the silence and the meaning of our lives.'[1] As we begin to seek out the meditative functions of sound, we begin in silence where we can make the first space in which we can begin to hear fully.

EXERCISE 10.1 ESTABLISHING SILENCE

When you have managed to create your own silence, look at how it felt to you. Did you find the time positive or negative? Were you able to enjoy the absence of noise or did you just miss the experience of sound? Did you find it easy to gather your thoughts or were you able to let go of thinking for a while? How long did your silence last? Was it long enough for your needs? Will you be able to do this again? Do you want to create silence regularly? It is not coincidental that silence has always been part of the religious life. If you can, make it a small part of your life.

Listening

> The Yoga of listening is controlling your ego so that it does only hear what it wants to hear.
>
> Henry Skolimowski, *EcoYoga*

Listening is not the same as hearing. It is easy to hear without listening. Hearing is passive but listening is active. Listening is a skill. When we listen to something, whether a person or a piece of music, we give our active attention so that we listen for meaning. The human voice reveals as much through intonation and emphasis as through words. The subtle nuances that convey well-being or frustration, confidence or fear, contentment or anxiety, are to be found in sound rather than word. Politeness and social conformity easily mask what is really being said. A good listener will hear the meaning through the words and will relate to intent rather than content. True communication lies in listening not just hearing.

In the babble of daily life and social interaction, we have the capacity to screen out conversations, background noises and everyday sounds and yet we can instantly focus on a crying child or our own name. If we have subconsciously screened out all that we do not want to hear, how can we be sure that we are hearing all that we really need to hear? Buddhism teaches mindfulness in all simple, ordinary activities. This concept can be helpfully employed to gauge our capacity to hear and listen with full attention.

The sounds of Nature

May all embodied creatures
Uninterruptedly hear
The sound of Dharma issuing from birds and trees,
Beams of light and even space itself.

From *The Shantiveda*

The sounds of technology have obscured the sounds of Nature. The sounds of technology cannot heal. There is no comfort in mechanical clatter, in electrical chatter or in the tapping of the keyboard. These are the sounds of work, the voice of commerce and the world of the marketplace. There is no healing for the soul here. Yet these are the sounds we value; these are the status symbols of our success. Now imagine for a moment the sound of waves pouring onto a shingle beach. Can you hear the rasp as wave and beach embrace briefly? Can you hear the flutter of stones being carried and turned? Can you hear the crash as a deeper wave drops onto water before rushing towards the shore? These sounds are deeply ingrained within us, whether from the memory of childhood or even some deeper ancestral memory; we respond to this ancient and primordial sound of nature. Not only does this sound relax and soothe but it seems to strip away the veneer of modernity in an instant. We are touched by a deeper current, for the waves broke upon the beach long before our most distant ancestors stood and heard the same sound. Nature has many sounds but unless we make an effort to hear them, we will remain in the prison house of the technological and the industrial. When did you last hear water trickling over stone, leaves rustling in the breeze or bird song?

Hearing these sounds in the memory or imagination whets the appetite for the real encounter, so open your inner ear to Nature's many voices.

EXERCISE 10.3 NATURE'S VOICES

Decide to find an opportunity to listen to the sounds of the natural world in your own way. Take your inner silence to the garden, the park, the hillside, the town square, the country lane, the field and the pathway. Listen out for the sounds of the evening and listen out for the sounds of the morning. Open yourself to the life that you discover through the sounds of Nature.

Creative sound

You live in a world of sounds. Sounds heard and unheard; sounds musical and chaotic; sounds strange and familiar; sounds stressful and pleasing; sounds that shatter and sounds that heal.

Olivia Dewhurst-Maddock, *Sound as Therapy*

It is curious how often sound appears as a determining factor in creation myths. A Pawnee creation story is very typical:

The four powers sang in praise of trees and grassy plains, and a second great storm was generated, which made the earth green and covered with growing trees and plants. A third time they sang, and the flood of water from the storm filled the rivers and streams and caused them to flow. With the fourth chant, seeds sprang forth and germinated.[2]

In the tradition of the mythic storyteller, C.S. Lewis evokes the presence of Aslan, the cosmic singer who sings a world into being:

A voice had begun to sing. Sometimes it seemed to come from all directions at once. Sometimes he almost thought it was coming out of the earth beneath them. Its lower notes were deep enough to be the voice of the earth herself. There were no words ... Then two wonders happened at the same moment. One was that the voice was joined by other voices. The second wonder was that the blackness overhead, all at once, was blazing with stars. The new stars and the new voices began at exactly the same time. If you had heard it, as Digory did, you would have felt quite certain that it was the stars themselves which were singing and that the First Voice, the deep voice which had made the stars appear and sing.[3]

We are familiar with the words of Genesis. 'In the beginning was the word, and the word was with God and the word was God.'

The idea of creative sound long pre-dates our current scientific understanding. We know that sound is vibration. The often quoted work by Ernst Chladni provides a fascinating insight into the relationship between sound and form. He laid down the experimental principles of acoustics. Chladni observed a clear relationship between vibration and pattern. In his experiments, sand sprinkled onto metal plates reacted to the different notes of a violin bow. As the bow was stroked against the plate consistent patterns appeared. These plates and their patterns have subsequently been called Chladni disks. His work was followed by others, notably Hans Jenny who developed methods that permitted greater accuracy and measurement. Jenny found that electrical impulses upon crystal lattices provided precise measurement. He experimented with different substances including liquids, dyes, glycerine, powders and gels. Every medium produced patterns in response to vibration. Movement began, pattern took shape, and then symmetry appeared. Metamorphosis was constant as tone and note were varied. Increased pitch created complexity. Delicate patterns appeared on films of water in response to vibration. Regular lattice formations appeared in sheets of glycerine. His increasingly sophisticated experiments with metal plates and piezoelectric vibrations reveal mandala-like images, which contained a central point with circular forms.

With the creation of a new instrument, which Jenny called the tonoscope, these experiments were extended to observe the effect of the human voice. An electrostatic variant even translated music into form, making it possible to see the music of Mozart and watch the sonatas of Bach in continuous motion. Using the tonoscope, the vibrations of the human voice were imparted into various selected indicators via a diaphragm. It became possible to see the visible results of a melody, continuous conversation, the breath, a single sound or a word. When the tonoscope was used with patients suffering from speech difficulties, the difference between a pure sound and skewed sound was clearly evident. The visual feedback was used to good effect in correcting speech patterns. Above its therapeutic uses the tonoscope supports an old idea, namely that certain sounds correctly sounded convey particular vibrational qualities.

The sounded word

Om Mane Padme Hum.

Tibetan Mantra

The fascinating work of cymatics bridges sound and form. It renders the invisible visible. It shows us what we hear. It should open our mind to the infinite possibilities of sound as both healer and destroyer in the world in which we live. It takes us directly into the tradition of the word as sounded meditation. Sounded words or phrases are currently known as **mantras**. The ancient Egyptians referred to such words as *hekau*, meaning words of power. There are mantras of many kinds from simple syllables, to words and meaningful phrases. Each functions at more than one level simultaneously. It is possible to translate mantra but this only provides an intellectual understanding. The mantra is more than this as the tonoscope has so clearly revealed to us. Something beyond our rational comprehension takes place as the mantra is sounded. It has long been maintained that one of the secrets of the mantra lies in its correct sounding. This is given between teacher and pupil; it cannot be learned from the printed word. The tonoscope supports this. Not only do we see the vibrating effect of vowels taking visible shape but in a

figure 10.1   sound gives rise to form: the Shri yantra

staggering demonstration of an ancient truth, the mantra *OM* when correctly sounded produces the **Shri yantra** as its visible counterpart. The universal mantra, the sound of the eternal, produces cosmic creation.

Mantric meditation is far more than just the repetition of a word or phrase. Its power goes far beyond literal meaning. Although a mantra is most often short, this should not deceive us into believing it to be a simple construction. A seed is invariably small, but it can give birth to a mighty oak. Like any other type of meditation, the mantra serves as key within the psyche. It cannot be approached without preparation. Without conscious involvement, the mantra is reduced to a meaningless noise on the air. To repeat a mantra mindlessly is to create babble of the worst kind. All spiritual keys penetrate into the depths of being through an organic and gentle process of integration that begins intellectually but proceeds to the realm of intuition and finally lodges with the birth of insight. The mantra works in just this way too. It is possible to commence by learning the traditional correspondences that are attributed to each mantra. Until such correspondences pass from the intellect to the heart the learning remains no more than rote repetition. Until the qualities expressed by the mantra have been

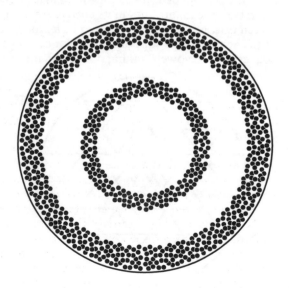

figure 10.2   the Circle of Life

internalized as living realities, the mantra remains as an empty vessel. For instance, the seed syllable 'O' is associated with an all round inclusive energy. It is called the universal energy. It represents the wholeness of things and stands for perfection. The tonoscope provides a powerful demonstration for us. The vowel 'O' when sounded correctly creates a circular form. Quite simply sounding the 'O' brings something new into being; 'In the beginning was the word.'

EXERCISE 10.4 THE CIRCLE OF LIFE

When the reality behind the sound is invoked the mantra becomes a container where spiritual truth resides. To employ the mantra with consciousness is to drink from the well of living waters and be nourished. Try to get in touch with the power within this most primal of all sounds. First, meditate upon the circle. When you feel you have a grasp of its meaning move on to the sounding of the O itself. You are going to attempt to vibrate this sound rather than just speak it. Take a deep breath so that you can project a long sound. Practise until you feel a sense of vibration in the head when the sound is made.

The vowel sounds probably belong to the earliest stage in history. The sounds a, e, i, o, u constitute the most basic human sounds by expressing an inner polarity between the unrestrained energy of the abdomen and a tightening in the head. It is noticeable that vowel sounds frequently appear in the most ancient of mantras from different traditions. The three vowels, O, U, A, have great significance as the basic foundations of many Tibetan mantras. The 'O' represents the all inclusive, the perfect and the eternal. The long vowel 'U' is considered to be the sound of depth, which symbolizes the descent of the supramental into the human life. The sound 'A' represents the human quality of speech, thought and communication. Two further sounds extend the meaning of these three sounds. The 'H', which is the sound of the breath, adds the quality of the life force itself. The nasalized 'M', which stands between the openness of the vowels and the closure of the consonants, adds a state beyond duality. These three vowels and two consonants form the three key Tibetan mantras, OM, AH and HUM. Together these three mantras symbolize the three mysteries of body, speech and mind. To use these mantras with intent and awareness is to evoke the qualities of body, speech and mind at both personal and transpersonal levels. Such teachings cannot be fully conveyed except by an empowered teacher. To read about a mantra is to learn of its functions, but to be initiated into the mantra is quite another experience:

> OM represents the universal;
> AH represents the ideal;
> HUM represents the individual.

We see the same principle at work through the Hebrew language where single letters again represent ideas. We who use the word, both spoken and written, for mundane communication find it difficult to comprehend what truth lies behind the tradition of the sacred word. We sense that it stands beyond our normal frame of reference. We live only with a mundane alphabet. It is one of the first things learned by a child in school. The alphabet is clearly important; it is elementary to written communication, but it hardly merits a spiritual status! Yet elsewhere and in other times the alphabet has indeed been seen as the vehicle for spiritual realization. The hieroglyphic language of the Egyptians was more properly called *Medu Neter*, meaning 'the sacred signs'. Hebrew remains a living spiritual language, as does Sanskrit. The difference between the alphabet as the mundane component of written word and as a tool of spiritual thought is simple and clear. The letters of the mundane alphabet carry no connotation other than just sound, whereas the individual letters of any sacred alphabet are themselves symbols. Individual letters serve as a code to convey meaning and words serve as philosophical concepts. Particular words come to carry significance. This significance is further emphasized when the written word becomes the sounded word. When the sacred written word is lifted from the page to become the sacred sounded word, it takes on a new dimension; it becomes a mantra. A few letters in combination can express a complete philosophy. We find this in the Tetragrammaton, the holy name of God, Yahweh. Such reverence is paid to this name that it is never spoken aloud. The four letters that make up this name are *Yod*, *He* and *Vau*, and the fourth letter *He* is repeated but it is differentiated by being marked as the *He* final. Each of the letters corresponds to one of the elements and to a level of creation:

The letter *Yod* represents the Element of Fire and the World of Archetypes;

The letter *He* represents the Element of Water and the World of Creation;

The letter *Vau* represents the Element of Air and the World of Formation;

The *He* final represents the Element of Earth and the World of Action.

In this way, saying the name of God encapsulates an entire philosophy and schema of creation as the divine impulse moves from the archetypal world to the world of action and physical results. The Sanskrit mantra, *Aum*, functions in a similar way. The first three letters are called the three quarters. The fourth quarter is the hidden quarter. It appears as vibration when the M is sounded. The Sanskrit symbol for the *Aum* is sometimes called the first mantra. The long lower curve represents the dream state and the upper left curve represents the waking state. The central curve projecting to the right represents the dreamless sleep between them. The crescent on the upper right symbolizes the veil of illusion and the dot stands for the transcendent state:

The A is attributed to Brahman the Creator;
The U is attributed to Vishnu the Preserver;
The M is attributed to Shiva the Destroyer.

There are many mantras of differing kinds and purposes. Divine names become mantra-like as invocations of the most sublime, the most holy, the highest power imaginable. Every tradition has its own sacred names, whether as the One or as many. Sufi practice includes the remembrance of God through the repetition of the divine name, this is **dhikr**. In Judaism, another monotheistic tradition, repeating the Tetragrammaton silently and inwardly remains a central practice. The name of Jesus forms the substance of the Jesus prayer. The instructions given to the early Christians in the *Philokalia* have much in common with esoteric disciplines. Heart, mind, breath, word and intent become as one: 'Collect your mind, lead it into the path of the breath, along which the air

figure 10.3   the first mantra, *Aum*

enters in, constrain it to enter the heart together with the inhaled air, and keep it there. Keep it there, but do not leave it silent and idle. Instead give it the following prayer; Lord Jesus Christ son of God, have mercy on me.'

Suzanne Segal provides us with a modern account that revolves around mantra. Her first encounters with mantra began entirely spontaneously:

> I used to meditate on my name. As a child of seven or eight I would sit cross-legged, eyes closed, on a long white couch in my parent's living room and say my name over and over to myself. The name would reverberate in my mind and with each repetition, starting off solid and strong. My name, who I was. Then fainter, repeating, repeating, repeating, until a threshold was crossed and the identity as that name broke, like a ship released suddenly from its mooring to float untethered on the ocean waves. Vastness appeared.

Vastness was to reappear in Suzanne's life in the most literal and extraordinary sense. She and the Void encountered each other. Her collision with the infinite began with mantra:

> I kept repeating the mantra out aloud until he instructed me to begin saying it more softly and then just silently I closed my eyes and started meditating. After a few minutes, I could feel myself settling down. Within a few minutes, I knew I would meditate for the rest of my life. Sitting in that chair repeating that Sanskrit word to myself in my mind, I was tenderly drawn into the embrace of my beloved silence.[4]

Her journey into vastness began with mantra and testifies to mantra as awakener. In some totally non-rational manner, mantras serve to awaken and to stimulate, to rouse the dormant and the latent. Mantras of awakening are attributed to six of the seven chakras. To vibrate the mantra correctly is to create change in the chakra itself. The mantras for the chakras are:

Base chakra: *Lam*
Sacral chakra: *Vam*
Solar plexus chakra: *Ram*
Heart chakra: *Yam*
Throat chakra: *Ham*
Brow chakra: *Om*

Mantras have acquired a mixed reputation, probably because a secret is implied in their nature. It is not possible to read a mantric word aloud and expect any of the results attributed to it.

Lama Govinda defines the nature and function of mantra for us:

> Mantras are neither magic spells whose inherent power
> can defy the laws of nature, nor are they formulas for
> psychiatric therapy or self hypnosis. They do not possess
> any power of their own, but are means for arousing and
> concentrating already existing forces in the human
> psyche. They are archetypal sound and word symbols
> that have their origin in the very structure of
> consciousness. They are therefore not arbitrary creations
> of individual initiative, but arise from the collective or
> general human experience, modified only by cultural or
> religious traditions.[5]

Sogyal Rinpoche speaks about a particular mantra. He says:

> The mantra I recommend to my students is OM HUM VAJRA
> GURU PADMA SIDDHI HUM. This is the mantra of
> Padmasambhava, the mantra of all Buddhas, Masters and
> realized beings. It is a force for transformation,
> protection and healing. ... A few years ago, I was
> conducting a workshop for three hundred people in
> Lyons, France. By the end of the afternoon I was
> completely drained, and a dull heavy atmosphere had
> descended over the whole room so I chanted this mantra
> I have taught you here. I was amazed by the effect; in a
> few moments I felt all my energy was restored, the
> atmosphere around us was transformed and the whole
> audience seemed once again bright and enchanting.[6]

He reminds us that mantra means that which protects the mind.
Each syllable is impregnated with spiritual power, condenses a
spiritual truth and vibrates with the blessings of the Buddhas.
These words should remind us that mantra is to be taken seriously.

The sacred voice

> The release of sound creates space in one's being.
> Mark Malachi, *Opening the Inner Gates*

Have you heard Tibetan monks in unified chant? The sounds
are unearthly and quite extraordinary. Low base notes bring a
vibrating presence. Sound billows and spreads like palpable
vapour. This is not song. It is resonating power. It is vibration.
As the sound draws us in, we become entrained and begin to
vibrate in harmony. This is the power in sound: it haunts and
mesmerizes, astounds and changes us simultaneously. The sacred
voice has a long and ancient lineage. It is still alive in cultures less

dominated by the pressures of commercial music. Make an effort to hear some of the sacred music and songs of the ages. These can awaken you in a way that populist music of the transient moment can never do. Discover the sacred chant which is neither quite song nor prayer. It continues as a living tradition having survived the test of time. By definition, sacred chant is never trivial or without meaning. There is no need for narrative verse or vocal virtuosity. The single word or short phrase is sufficient to encapsulate devotion, worship, identification or praise. It gains in power through repetition as mind, heart and voice affirm the same intent over and over. Every tradition selects its own sacred words and phrases in accordance with its beliefs and aspirations. These are the divine names, the sacred sounds and words of power, the words that are always meant to be sounded, not spoken, vibrated not verbalized.

Take courage in both hands, believe that your own voice has meaning and power. Be experimental with your own voice. Sounds are deeply related to every aspect of human life. The cooing of a contented baby, the sounds of laughter and the wailing of grief are instinctual responses. Releasing sound releases deeply embedded emotion. Use your own sound to release the blocked and the outworn within you.

Be open to possibilities: sing, shout, chant, vibrate, intone, listen, hear and discover the power of sound for yourself.

EXERCISE 10.5 LET IT GO

Before commencing the meditation, become aware of any identifications you want to shed, so you may want to spend time getting in touch with these. Then become focused on qualities that you want to be identified with. Name the way in which you want others to see you.

On the inbreath, take in the new identity by affirming what you want for yourself. Use smooth, soft and harmonious sounds to accompany the drawing in of your new being. On the outbreath release energy using any sounds that naturally arise, just let them come out. These noises are most likely to be sharp, loud and high pitched. Continue the breathing cycle and just allow sounds to emerge from each outbreath. Once the process of healing is in motion do not be surprised at the sounds that issue from you. Shrieks, shouts and noises may erupt. You will know when you are emptied. At the close hum gently to settle yourself.

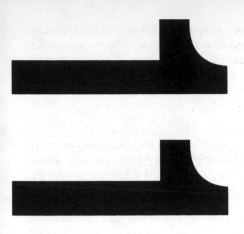

growing: the paradox of selfhood

In this chapter you will learn:

- about different models of reality
- about an Egyptian model
- about the mystical model
- about a quantum model.

Our newest revelations from researchers all over the
world are forcing us to take a closer look at who we are
physically, mentally and spiritually.

Stanislav Grof, *The Holotrophic Mind*

Who am I?

Who has not pondered this question? Where can we look for
an answer? It is not a simple question and we should not expect
a simple answer. The way we define ourselves is constrained by
the models at our disposal. Models of the individual are closely
connected to the models we hold of the world at large. Every
major religious tradition, both ancient and modern, has offered
a template for becoming. The template has crucial significance
for the individual as it becomes the way of moving forward
into life. A mechanistic view of the world provides a
mechanistic view of the individual. A holistic overview permits
the emergence of a holistic view of self. A divisive template
divides the individual in consequence. There is no doubt of the
power of the template to create its own reality as social
institutions are in turn shaped by its influence. How we define
ourselves is in many ways a reflection of the template we accept
and internalize. Absolutes are few and templates change too.
Exoteric religious models have always been prescriptive of
external behaviour. Esoteric models have provided ways and
means of going beyond the very same prescriptions. Mystical
models have always revealed the essential unity of the
individual and the whole. In the West we are still touched by a
largely prescriptive model. Its esoteric possibilities have been
veiled and its mystical moments have never been translated
into a teaching lineage. An impoverished model creates
impoverished lives but a rich model creates rich lives. As we
seek to define ourselves, we cannot deny the many complexities
of being human. Our experience of being is highly paradoxical,
we sense both constancy and change. We recognize both
identity and transformation. We have a sense of the journey in
life through experience, yet the journey is not linear but multi-
dimensional.

The long standing Western template has turned a paradox into
schism. Nature and spirit have long been divided one from the
other. Body and soul have been set against each other as
competing forces. Heaven and earth themselves have been
divided. Earthly life has been relegated to a poor second when

viewed against an eternity in glory. This model offers only a much weighted choice. Where can the paradoxical self find a footing when the two worlds have been set so firmly against each other? Here is a closed model with stark choices and no place for becoming; it offers no integrated psychology.

In yet another example of schism even Western psychology is largely clinically based and unwilling to approach the transcendent. We seek wholeness in partial templates only at our peril and a great accommodation is required. We pay a high price for such salvation because we lose touch with meaning when personal growth is stunted or, worse still, not permitted. Arthur Deikman, himself a psychotherapist, recognizes the barrenness of the models that might be nourished by psychotherapy: 'Western psychotherapy is hard put to meet human beings' need for meaning, for it attempts to understand clinical phenomena in a framework, based on scientific materialism, in which meaning is arbitrary and purpose non-existent.'[1] However, we do not have to be dependent or reliant upon models that have already shown themselves to be flawed. New models will rise as times change. The family therapist Virginia Satir anticipates the future: 'We have yet to see what the flowering of the human being can be like and now is the time. The next century is a very important century where human beings will be looked at in terms of who they really are.'[2]

Of course, who we really are is a fundamental question. What is a human being? Looking at a person in terms of who they are places significance on the immediate moment, not the future. We only have the moment, we do not have the future. Templates that place meaning only in the future deny the present and the future as envisaged never comes. Whether that future is a heavenly paradise, eternal glory or an ascended existence, the result is the same. The moment in hand evaporates in the face of a future which exists only within a particular belief system. Meditation places awareness in the moment itself. There is nothing more to learn beyond that. This simple truth liberates us from everything except the present moment and the awareness of it. Let us find ourselves here and now in this very moment.

The following meditation deliberately presents a traditional meditation but in an unusual form. It is normally presented as a series of disidentifications which culminate in creating distance from body, emotion and thought. Its culminating realization is a centre of pure consciousness. Although the testimony of Suzanne Segal shows the truth of this, in the light of current New Age language, this meditation is so often misunderstood. The words imply that 'pure consciousness' is no more than a vague, woolly, disembodied spirit. The disidentification process has meaning when disidentification has taken place. Having read Segal's account, you can undertake the meditation in its more traditional form with understanding. You are the person you identify yourself to be. In relative reality, if you identify with mind, body, emotion and consciousness as a unity, then it is true for you. This is the perspective of Jivatman, embodied consciousness. If you identify with the Absolute this is **Atman**, the universal consciousness. This is the paradox of being – both realities are true at the same moment in time.

EXERCISE 11.1 I AM WHO I AM

Sit quietly in meditation. Become aware of your breath. Settle into a rhythm that is comfortable to you. Begin to meditate on the breath itself. As you breathe in feel yourself receiving from the universal. As you breathe out there is a giving back to the universal. With each breath there is an exchange between the personal and the transpersonal. Be aware of the breath within your body. When you wish, move your awareness into your body. Use your hands to touch your own flesh. Just place your hands anywhere, but with awareness. Affirm your own physicality. Then begin to place your awareness inside the body under the skin. Here you will find muscles and tendons, ligaments and tissue. Descend deeper into the body, where you will find nerves, arteries and veins all in a state of constant activity. Take your awareness as deeply into the body as you can. Acknowledge the work of chemical exchange and the individual organs in relation to one another. Acknowledge the constant activity and renewal taking place within yourself. Take your awareness into your bones, which are red with blood. Go into the bones, where blood is made. Go on and make your own discoveries. Finally just affirm, 'This is me. I own it all.' With awareness place your hand on your stomach and move into memory and begin to recall all range of emotions that you have known. You may find that memories of particular incidents appear in your mind. As each incident and emotion is recalled, once more affirm, 'This is me. I own it all.' When this phase is completed, with awareness just lightly touch the forehead with a finger. Reflect on the capacity of your mind for reason, judgement, memory, intuition and insight. Reflect on all the abilities you can name. When you feel this phase is over, affirm, 'This is me. I own it all.' Finally place your hand over your heart and become aware of your heartbeat. Just open your heart to life beyond your own. Open yourself to connection and once more affirm, 'This is me, I own it all.'

This simple meditation affirms the whole self as experienced in the moment. You do not have to look for yourself in the future because you are here right now. Spirituality is not a distant concept, a goal for tomorrow or even a future life. You affirm your spiritual nature by being whole and fully present. Healing is derived from the Anglo-Saxon word *hal* and *holy* which means to make whole or restore. When you sense your wholeness there is no sense of a breach within. Meditation can maintain your sense of wholeness. Sheldon Kramer writes, 'For me spirituality came alive through the practice of meditation. Through regular meditation practice there is a feeling of connection, a oneness and a vivacious energy state.'[3]

In affirming oneness within, we also sense a connection to the greater whole, for holism places us in a relationship to everything. As Virginia Satir wishes, 'One of my hopes is that you will be able to look at any small piece and see the whole. Any single cell of you contains your whole pattern and by that same definition every one of us contains the whole world.'[4] This realization, not as an intellectual construct but as an immediate and total knowing, lies at the heart of the mystical revelation. The total nature of this self-revelation may well be the enlightenment experience. The answer to the question, 'Who am I?' may prove to be 'You are the whole universe' – a paradox indeed, for many of us are ill-prepared to cope with that realization in the day-to-day world of relative reality. Nevertheless, for some the greater whole does become the self-identification.

The mystical moment

Often confused with religion, the mystical tradition occupies a place of its own.

Arthur Deikman, *The Observing Self*

In order to clarify our understanding of the relationship between religion and mysticism, we may construct a model composed of three concentric circles. The outer circle represents a religious tradition as a whole. It is by definition the largest of the three containers and it also represents the religion as social and cultural container. It holds all the accumulated dogma, teaching, moral codes and outer observances. Within this we find a considerably smaller circle, which represents the esoteric practices of the tradition. The emphasis here is upon personal growth, unfoldment and self-development. Here lies the possibility of deeper personal experience. Within this again lies a third and considerably smaller circle representing the mystical encounter which is always possible. This inner circle belongs to the tradition as a whole but, at the same time, it is often constituted as a tradition of its own. Here the fruits of accumulated experience are transformed once again into a completely new dimension. For it is here the small self and the universal self become one in consciousness.

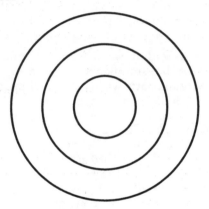

figure 11.1   three in one – paths to the centre

This model might also help us to view the self as once more we ask the question, 'Who am I?' The writer Isha Schwaller de Lubicz, a guide to the mysticism of Ancient Egypt, offers a tripartite self – the Automaton, the Permanent Witness and the Spiritual Witness. The Automaton refers to life lived automatically, without reference to any self-conscious development. We can relate this to the exoteric path, which provides general codes, dogmas and beliefs to live by. The Permanent Witness arises through practices, such as mindfulness, which develop self-awareness. Its characteristic factor is an interior quality of detachment. The third container represents the true ground of universal being where the personal self has ceased: the Spiritual Witness is the pure consciousness that watches. Paradoxically, the Real Self proves to be not a separate self at all but the whole.

Continuing the model presented by Isha Schwaller de Lubicz, we see two opposing forces at work. The shift from the wants of the personality to the wants of the spiritual witness constitutes the work of the spiritual path. This transfer of identification can be accomplished in many ways.

The personality wants:

- continuity on earth
- the relative values of this temporary existence
- intellectual information put at the services of worldly interests both social and scientific, or commercial career
- mediocrity – since rash extremes can never win public approval and gain social and worldly advantages
- utilitarianism, meaning everything that fits in with mundane computations and logical reasons.

However, the spiritual witness desires:

- to unite with the human and thus transmute it into an eternal being
- absolute values that are indestructible
- to open the 'heart' to intuitive knowledge
- the sense of 'excess' as a springboard from which to overleap human limitations and convert the fall of man into an opportunity of evolution
- unalterable love of reality
- love of life for its own sake
- love of impersonal love.[5]

The Maharishi describes three stages in the identification with the transcendent field. He calls these states Cosmic Consciousness, God Consciousness and Unity Consciousness. Cosmic consciousness is characterized by the emergence of the spiritual witness, the watcher on high. This awareness watches while remaining quite detached from all phenomena, remaining awake even while the body sleeps. In the state of God Consciousness the whole world is seen to be imbued with sacredness. Here the spiritual witness now disappears. Finally, there is Unity Consciousness.

The distinction between the ordinary self and the real self appears to make little sense. It is not a new idea, but one that pervades religious literature of every tradition. Hinduism refers to the self as the Atman, which is immortal, constant, unchanging and unbounded. *The Crest Jewel of Wisdom* describes Atman as 'that by which the universe is pervaded, which nothing pervades, which causes all things to shine but which all things cannot make shine'. The mystical experience does not belong to the past but to the present. Suzanne Segal, who had used her own name as a mantra at the age of seven, describes her long and painful spiritual awakening in the book *Collision with the Infinite*. Her childhood knowing deepened into serious interest in spirituality. During a retreat, she began to experience her first encounter with the transcendent field:

> I was gripped by a tremendous power like a huge magnet that pulled me into a tunnel of light at infinite speed. At the same time, the tunnel itself expanded outwards at infinite speed with a tumultuous roar that rose with ear-slitting crescendo as the infinity exploded in light. The moment of explosion marked the crossing of a threshold. In an increment of time too small to be measured the blaze of some invisible inferno engulfed everything, turning all phenomena inside out exposing the underside of all creation, emptiness.

This was just the beginning: 'My mode of perceiving had been jarred out of its ordinary pattern. It was impossible to focus separately on objects because boundaries between them had receded into the background, supplanted by a luminosity so powerful that everything in the visual field appeared to melt together into one large radiant mass.' These experiences culminated in a massive and bizarre episode in the most ordinary of circumstances. While standing at a bus stop, she experienced a complete disassociation of consciousness, seeing everything from the place of an outside witness. Understandably, she experienced total panic. The witnessing persisted for months and each moment was excruciating. She feared for her sanity. Finally, the witness too disappeared, making an unbearable situation even more frightening: 'The witness had at least held a location for me albeit a distant one. In the dissolution of the witness there was literally no more experience of a me at all.' She concludes, 'The experience of a personal identity switched off and was never to appear again.' Can you imagine coping with daily life while in this state of awareness? Curiously, Segal reports that outwardly no one could see any difference as everything carried on normally. Twelve years later she experienced another transition, this time to Unity Consciousness. The personal self was completely gone. She was living in the Zen state of No-I.[6]

Segal's account of her long walk with emptiness is both fascinating and terrifying. Despite numerous attempts by therapists, no one managed to cure her. The emptiness could not be removed. How does Suzanne Segal who is not Suzanne Segal, except on identifying pieces of paper, live in the ordinary world? She says, 'This life is now lived in a constant, ever present awareness of the infinite vastness that I am in. In this state there is absolutely no reference point, yet an entire range of emotions, thoughts, actions and responses are simultaneously present.' She now works as a psychologist. Few would wish to walk where she has been but perhaps we can take something from her journey. In the light of her own revelation she looks at the identities we construct for ourselves from information and inference of others: 'I begin with everyone by asking them to tell me who they take themselves to be.' Perhaps this is what we may learn from her collision with the infinite. We can become the person others impose upon us or we can become the person we choose to be. How do you wish to be seen? How shall you be identified now, and where are you identified? We began with the question 'Who are you?' When asked this same question, Suzanne Segal answers, 'When I am asked who I am, the only possible answer is I am the infinite, the vastness, the substance of all things. I am no one and everyone.' Here is paradox on a grand scale. Who are you?

EXERCISE 11.2 FALSE LABELS

Take time to locate some of the identifications that others have projected onto you. What names and labels have you identified with? What labels have you carried from parents and siblings? Bringing them into consciousness is the first step to ridding yourself of these skins that you have inhabited. There may be a few or there may be many. You will need to decide at what pace you wish to look at them. Also decide whether you wish to just rid yourself of the old or whether you are ready to replace it with a new one.

When you have identified a projected identity, imagine yourself in a skin-tight garment. See the words that have been used against you written all over the garment. When you are ready, unzip the garment and allow yourself to stand naked for a moment. If you wish to take on a new identity, visualize a garment that expresses what you want. Let it be loose fitting so that you can get used to it gradually. If you have no clear view of a self-chosen identity just put on a soft white robe. Do not leave yourself naked.

The mystical state

> Not only has mysticism its fount in what is the raw material of all religion, but also all the most profound insights of religious truth have their origin in the mystical experience of those who have led the spiritual progress of the human race.
>
> F.C. Happold, *Mysticism*

The mystical experience is well documented throughout history right up to the present time. Sporadic moments of mystical breakthrough of lesser degrees seem not uncommon. According to the Religious Experience Unit at Oxford Surveys, 36 per cent of the English survey group and 43 per cent of the American survey group reported a mystical experience. However, without further explanation of content it is difficult to know exactly what is meant in this instance. Such breakthroughs are often briefly experienced and not repeated. Despite being short lived, such moments of high intensity have the power to effect great personal change. The mystical state is characterized by:

- *Ineffability*: the mystical state defies expression in terms that are fully intelligible through the intellect. Its quality and nature cannot be conveyed through words. It is impossible adequately to convey meaning through mere words, which can only fall short of the experience.
- *Noetic quality*: the mystical state imparts **gnosis**, that is a direct knowing, which brings tremendous immediate insight into the fundamental nature of reality.
- *Transiency*: the mystical state is rarely sustained. Sometimes it is extremely brief, lasting no more than a matter of moments, or it can be extended to hours and has been witnessed to last for several days. It does not replace ordinary life. The return to ordinary consciousness is often painful, like moving from light back into darkness. Knowing the difficulties of this return, Buddhists stress the importance of developing equanimity.

- *Passivity*: in the mystical state the self, which has control in the ordinary world feels suspended. The state comes and goes according to a volition outside conscious control.
- *Universal consciousness*: the world of form is experienced as a unity, though the intensity of the experience diminishes after the return to ordinary world, a sense of connection and participation remains.
- *Timelessness*: the mystical state conveys a sense of timelessness.
- *Transparency of ego*: the experience brings absolute certainty that the ego is not the real self.[7]

These characteristics are quite unlike the defining features of rational waking consciousness with which we so easily identify. This is the template we choose to live out. At some future time a radically different template of universal wholeness may become the norm, but for the present we have a variety of models to choose as personal templates.

Models of self

> Western psychotherapy, in basing itself almost exclusively on the world view of scientific materialism, has impoverished its model of human consciousness and lost the meaning and significance of human life.
>
> Arthur Deikman, *The Observing Self*

Models are only models, that is all. Each model should be judged by its results in terms of human meaning. Ancient models served different cultural conditions. New models will arise. The system of Psychosynthesis, developed by Robert Assagioli, is one of the few Western psychological systems that recognize the need for a transcendent dimension to human life. Assagioli names, 'Another vast realm of our inner being which has been for the most part neglected by the science of psychology although its nature and its human value are of superior quality. The reason for such a curious neglect would in itself constitute an interesting piece of psychoanalysis and would shed much light on the psychology of psychologists.'[8] The strength of his system lies in its graded structure and its progressive introduction to the transcendent realm. Here is a Western, graduated path to self-realization. A graduated structure offers security and integration strategies as we move from one level of identification to another. Shedding one set of labels and its accompanying identity is a fraught process. This is quite literally the way in which we give birth to the new self-chosen identity. The contemporary writer on human consciousness, Ken Wilbur, restates an ancient truth for the modern reader. 'We have to "die" to our false, separate self in order to awaken to our immortal and transcendent self.'⁹

Searching for the self

> The basic difference between our Western psychology and the mystical tradition lies in our assumptions about the self.
>
> Arthur Deikman, *The Observing Self*

A sequence of Taoist paintings and texts depict the very quest that we share. Nobody knows how these paintings first came to exist. Early versions show a series of five pictures. By the twelfth century these had been extended to eight. The Chinese Master, Kakuan, then proceeded to add two extra paintings. The Taoist sequence finished with the experience of the Void, but Master Kakuan added a picture to represent the return to the world. He symbolized this as the marketplace. The Taoist schema has much in common with the Tibetan scheme, the Nine Stages of Mental Quiescence, which takes taming an elephant as its theme. Unlike Segal, the seeker in this tableau sets out to seek the vastness. Segal was engulfed by the vastness and taken unawares.

The search for the bull

Desolate through forest and
    fearful in jungles
he is seeking an Ox which he
    does not find.
Up and down dark, nameless,
    wide-flowing rivers,
in deep mountain thickets he
    treads many bypaths.
Bone-tired, heart-weary, he
    carries on his search
for this something which he yet
    cannot find.
At evening he hears cicadas
    chirping in the trees.

(a) The seeker is exhausted but does not give up

figure 11.2   searching for the bull

Finding the tracks

Innumerable footprints he has
  seen
in the forest along the water's
  edge.
Over yonder does he see the
  trampled grass?
Even the deepest gorges of the
  topmost mountains
can't hide this Ox's nose which
  reaches right to heaven.

(b) The seeker finds the trail at last

First glimpse of the Ox

A nightingale warbles on a
  twig,
the sun shines on undulating
  willows.
There stands the Ox, where
  could he hide?
That splendid head, those
  stately horns,
what artists could portray
  them?

(c) The Source is present in every
activity. Awareness must be properly
focused to realize this

Catching the Ox

He must tightly grasp the
  rope and not let it go,
for the Ox still has unhealthy
  tendencies.
Now he charges up to the
  highlands,
now he loiters in a misty
  ravine.

(d) Despite some progress, the mind of the
seeker is still easily distracted

Taming the Ox

He must hold the noose-rope
    tight and not allow the Ox
    to roam,
lest off to muddy haunts it
    should stray.
Properly tended, it becomes
    clean and gentle.
Untethered, it willingly
    follows its master.

(e) The seeker must continue to apply the noose-rope which is meditation in order to prevent the Ox from straying

Riding the Ox home

Riding free as air he buoyantly
    comes home
through evening mists in wide
    straw-hat and cape.
Wherever he may go he
    creates a fresh breeze,
while in his heart a profound
    tranquillity prevails.
This Ox requires not a blade of
    grass.

(f) The struggle for control is over

Ox forgotten, self alone

Only on the Ox was he able
    to come Home,
but lo, the Ox is now
    vanished, and alone and
    serene
sits the man.
The red sun rides high in the
    sky as he dreams placidly.
Yonder beneath the thatched
    roof
his idle whip and rope are
    lying.

(g) The whip and rope are now put to one side. There is nothing more to catch

Both Ox and self forgotten

Whip, rope, Ox and man alike
belong to Emptiness.
So Vast and infinite the azure
sky
that no concept of any sort
can reach it.
Over a blazing fire a
snowflake cannot survive.
When this state of mind is
realised
comes at last comprehension
of the spirit of the ancient
Patriarchs.

(h) The Void is realized

Returning to the source

He has returned to the Origin
come back to the Source,
but his steps have been taken
in vain.
It is as though he were now
blind and deaf.
Seated in his hut, he hankers
not for things outside.
Streams meander on of
themselves,
red flowers naturally bloom
red.

(i) A state of Oneness is fully realized

**Entering the marketplace
with helping hands**

Barechested, barefooted, he
comes into the market
place.
Muddied and dust covered,
how broadly he grins!
Without recourse to mystic
powers,
withered trees he swiftly
brings to bloom.

(j) The seeker returns to the world enlightened
and transformed[10]

No boundaries

> The ultimate metaphysical secret, if we dare state it, is
> simply that there are no boundaries in the universe.
>
> Ken Wilbur, *No Boundaries*

We live at a most extraordinary time in the history of the
world. Mystics have long made particular claims about the
nature of an ultimate or absolute level of reality. Such claims
would have baffled the Newtonian scientists of the past.
However, science in the quantum age finds itself increasingly
in agreement with the stated mystical view. Contemporary
physicists show us a world at odds with the evidence of our
senses. Schrodinger expresses it very simply for us:

> Our experience tells us that the physical world is solid,
> real and independent of us. Quantum mechanics says
> simply that this is not so.[11]

Only now has yet another particle been discovered that lives
for only a millionth of a billionth of a second. This is the
underpinning of the universe. Our familiar world of
appearances, which is the world of form and phenomena,
exists upon a deeper stratum, which would be unfamiliar and
extraordinary if our senses were able to record this
simultaneously. Here is perhaps the ultimate paradox:

> Quantum theory demolishes some cherished common-
> sense concepts about the nature of reality. By blurring
> the distinction between subject and object, cause and
> effect, it introduces a strong holistic element into our
> world-view. The question is, how to bridge the divide
> between these two levels, the microscopic and the
> macroscopic; how can we hold on to our everyday view
> of things as intrinsically separate in time and space
> whilst at the same time accepting that under the surface,
> as it were, all things are apparently interconnected in
> some sea of holism.[12]

Deikman concludes that, 'The universe newly discovered by
modern physics is characterized by unity, simultaneity, and
human consciousness as an interacting dimension of that
world.'[13] This is the heart of the mystical paradigm. While
science is happy to contemplate holism, a neutral concept that
appears to be free from the accumulated baggage of the ages,
it remains uncomfortable with too close a pursuit of the
mystical; much rests on this fine distinction. What difference
might there be between a holistic philosophy and a mystical

philosophy, a holistic world-view and a mystical world-view. The march of holism will surely continue at an accelerating pace as the West continues to be fascinated by the processes of the bubble chamber and the particle accelerator. The results will be cumulative and highly significant. The model we create of the whole will shape the template we collectively offer to the individual. The real message here is that you are whatever you accept you wish to be.

12

waking: the enlightenment breakthrough

In this chapter you will learn:
- about the possibility of enlightenment
- about personal experiences of enlightenment.

Let me show how far our nature is enlightened or unenlightened.

Plato, *Book VII*

Waking up

In Plato's *Republic* we are presented with an allegory of the human condition. Human beings live underground in a cave. They have lived in the cave since childhood, chained at the legs and necks. They know no other existence. In the cave a fire blazes. Between the fire and the prisoners there is a raised way with a low wall. Free men pass through behind the low wall but the chained prisoners do not see them directly, only as shadows cast by firelight. The prisoners mistake these reflections for reality. We are loathe to admit that we might be the prisoners in the cave. Our lives are not spent chained in the darkness and confusion. Our lives are filled with busy activity and full schedules and we are too busy to be confused! It is difficult to think of the waking life as the sleeping life from which we must awaken in order that we may live. Stop, look around at the people you know and the people you see. Is it possible that you walk with sleepwalkers? Do you sleep or wake? Is it possible that we all live like sleepwalkers in a dream. Though common sense may reel at the idea, spiritual tradition universally proclaims it. The Hasidic teacher, Rabbi Nachman, said, 'People may be asleep all their lives. But through tales told by a true holy one, they can be awakened.'[1]

Many spiritual stories are about waking up. The verb *buddha* means to wake up. One who wakes up is called a **Buddha**. It is difficult to accept the idea that we sleepwalk through life's many circumstances, yet it is a universal and age-old idea. Dreams are often confused and sometimes bizarre, frequently haphazard and occasionally powerful and dramatic. The dream tantalizes too as we struggle to grasp fragments that seem to convey a sense of meaning to us through symbol and metaphor. How difficult it is to remember the dream in all its details as we leave the dream state for outer reality. In the tradition of the spirituality awakened, Osho writes, 'You are fast asleep, and you don't know who you are.'[2] How difficult it is to recall the details of ordinary waking life through the filter of ordinary consciousness. Do you remember the conversations that you have undertaken in the past with friends, family, colleagues and opponents? How many special moments in your life do you remember? How many ordinary times can you recall? What were you thinking about yesterday mid-morning? What was the nature of your life aspiration a year ago?

The spiritual life is ever about paradox and the shattering of a world created upon the evidence of the common senses. We find ourselves on the horns of this dilemma once more. Is it even possible that waking life can be compared to a dream from which we are asked to awaken? How can we awaken? What are we waking from? We are awake every day, what more must we do. Waking consciousness is clearly one level of mind. It is largely dependent on the input of the five senses. Spiritual practice always seeks to loosen the grip of the five senses. When life is lived through the five sense alone, we create an internal map of the outside world based on sensory perceptions. The perceptual map, which enables us to negotiate ourselves through everyday life, also creates a screen that acts as a constant reference point. We do not see a new object as it is but in relation to our existing conceptual package. How confused we feel when presented with an object without a frame of reference; this is the-stock-in trade of guessing games. When we have no reference point, we are forced to examine any new object in the light of its own nature, rather than through a pre-existing model. The graduated path to enlightenment might be thought of as a conscious system for destructuring the perception system: 'The complexity of the brain tends to insulate us from the reality of pure consciousness surrounding us. As all meditation systems seem to concur, we "tune in" to pure consciousness by stilling the fruits of the brain's complexity.'[3] This conscious weakening of the internal model permits us to perceive directly without the screen of the inner conceptual world. The moment of enlightenment is most often experienced as a radical breakthrough, as if we see the world for the very first time. 'An experience which is not yet limited by preconceived ideas has all the qualities of infinity.'[4]

Every spiritual system recognizes the awakened state and refers to it in its own language. Zen calls this state **Mujodo no taigeu** which is No-Mind. In Tibetan Buddhism the ultimate awakened state is that of the *Bodhisattva*. In Theravadin Buddhism it is called *Arahantship*. In *Kabbalah* the goal of the journey is to become a **Devekut,** one who cleaves to God. The Transcendental Meditation movement recognizes **Cosmic Consciousness.** Sufis recognise the state called **Baqa** and Hindus speak of **Moksha,** which is liberation. Krishnamurti spoke of **Choiceless Awareness** and Gurdjieff spoke of **Objective Consciousness.** Christianity offers the model of **Christ Consciousness**. Buddhism offers the model of **Buddha Consciousness** and Hinduism offers the model of **Krishna Consciousness**. The variety of names and descriptions should not confuse us. The many practices and approaches should not deter us from glimpsing the central truth which resides here. The *Avatamsaka Sutra* says, 'The way of the Buddha is in the 84,000 doors of liberation.' In other words, the ways to liberation are without number. Why not expect and welcome many possibilities. Salute alternative paths, rejoice in variety and diversity. There are many spokes on a wheel but they all lead to the centre.

Enlightenment: the inner light

Every individual has the potentiality to become enlightened in the course of this life or later existences.

Lama Govinda, *Creative Meditation*

The symbol of light is frequently used in spiritual discourse and it is not difficult to understand the universality of this. Simply ask yourself what would you want most in a pitch-black room? Your answer will surely be 'light'. As light enables you to negotiate in the dark, so light represents the emergence of self-consciousness through the fruition of insight and the process of transformation.

EXERCISE 12.1 THE COMING OF LIGHT

Imagine yourself in a pitch-black place. The dark is so intense that you cannot see your hand before your eyes. You have no sense of direction. You feel disoriented in time and space. Your darkness compels you to dwell upon the light. You begin to yearn for light in the darkness. You begin to crave the possibility of light. The image of light begins to fill your mind. You think of nothing else, for there is nothing else you want more than light. As your thoughts become stronger and clearer you notice that the darkness around you seems somehow thinner and less dense. You hold the mind steady and continue to create the inner light. The darkness around you is receding. The space is lit by a pale glow. This is your light. What is your choice for the future, the light or the dark?

Light is often used as a metaphor for spiritual awakening. It serves well as a symbol for clarity and understanding. Sudden moments of great clarity are more than metaphorical and such breakthrough moments take place in reality as a matter of daily life. Sometimes these breakthroughs assume cataclysmic proportions and seem to shatter and simultaneously reshape our view of reality. We have talked about absolute and relative levels of consciousness. We have noted the nature of the exoteric, esoteric and mystical paths. We can all relate to a position of relative understanding. It is the common human condition. At the same time we can recognize that an experience of the absolute is also a human possibility. Not all seek the quantum leap of being, yet the experience remains. It is a signpost to those who seek a signpost. The experience of enlightenment is not confined to the great and famous mystics of history. This is a living reality that the ordinary person can also touch in the world of today. First-hand accounts of such experiences make compelling reading and the book *The Three Pillars of Zen* contains a number of such accounts, which can each add to our understanding of the enlightenment experience. The story rendered by a Canadian housewife is especially interesting as it details her intense struggle with the *koan*, Mu. After seven days of intense inner labour and spiritual incubation, she experienced her first enlightenment:

> The days and weeks that followed were the most deeply happy and serene of my life. There was no such thing as a 'problem'. Things were either done or not done, but in any case there was neither worry nor consternation. Past relationships to people who had once caused me deep disturbance I now saw with perfect understanding. For the first time in my life I was able to move like the air, in any direction, free at last from the self which had always been such a tormenting bond to me.

Some six years later she experienced a second awakening:

> One spring day as I was working in the garden, the air seemed to shiver in a strange way, as though the usual sequence of time had opened into a new dimension, and I became aware that something untoward was about to happen, if not that day then soon. Hoping to prepare in some way for it, I doubled my regular sittings of **Zazen** and studied Buddhist books late into each night.

> A few evenings later, after carefully sifting through *The Tibetan Book of the Dead* and then taking my bath, I sat in front of a painting of the Buddha and listened quietly by candlelight to a slow movement of Beethoven's A

Minor Quartet, a deep expression of man's self-renunciation, and then went to bed. The next morning, just after breakfast, I suddenly felt as though I were being struck by a bolt of lightning, and I began to tremble. All at once the whole trauma of my difficult birth flashed into my mind. Like a key, this opened dark rooms of secret resentments and hidden fears which flowed out of me like poisons. Tears gushed out and so weakened me I had to lie down. Yet a deep happiness was there. ... Slowly my focus changed:

'I'm dead! There's nothing to call *me*. There never was a *me*! It's an allegory, a mental image, a pattern upon which nothing was ever modelled.' I grew dizzy with delight. Solid objects appeared as shadows, and everything my eyes fell upon was radiantly beautiful. These words can only hint at what was revealed to me in the days that followed.

1 The world as apprehended by the senses is the least true (in the sense of complete), the least dynamic (in the sense of eternal movement), and the least important in a vast 'geometry of existence' of unspeakable profundity, whose rate of vibration, whose intensity and subtlety are beyond verbal description.

2 Words are cumbersome and primitive – almost useless in trying to suggest the true multi-dimensional workings of an indescribably vast complex of dynamic force, to contact which one must abandon one's normal level of consciousness.

3 The least act, such as eating or scratching an arm, is not at all simple. It is merely the visible movement in a network of causes and effects reaching forward into Unknowingness and back into an infinity of Silence where individual consciousness cannot even enter. There is truly nothing to know, nothing that can be known.

4 The physical world is an infinity of movement, of Time-Existence. But simultaneously it is an infinity of Silence and Voidness. Each object is thus transparent. Everything has its own special inner character, its own karma or 'life in time', but at the same time there is no place where there is emptiness, where one object does not flow into another.

5 The least expression of weather variations, a soft rain or a gentle breeze touches me as a – what can I say – miracle of unmatched wonder, beauty and goodness. There is nothing to do; just to be is a supremely total act.

6 Looking into faces, I see something of the long chain of their past existence, and sometimes something of the future. The past ones recede behind the outer face like ever-finer tissues, yet are at the same time impregnated in it.

7 When I am in solitude I can hear a 'song' coming forth from everything. Each and every thing has its own song; even moods, thoughts and feelings have their finer songs. Yet beneath this variety they intermingle in one inexpressible vast unity.

8 I feel a love which, without object, is best called lovingness. But my old emotional reactions still coarsely interfere with the expressions of this supremely gentle and effortless lovingness.

9 I feel a consciousness which is neither myself nor not of myself, which is protecting or leading me into directions helpful to my proper growth and maturity, and propelling me away from that which is against growth. It is like a stream into which I have flowed and joyously is carrying me beyond myself.[5]

Who among us can fail to be moved, even slightly disturbed, by this profound and dramatic experience? These states, which seem so far removed from the mundane world and the everyday aspiration of good folk, point to a potentiality that can be found in the human heart. This account clearly takes us from the mundane and the ordinary experience of daily life into extraordinary dimensions and unfamiliar perceptions; it would be tempting to dismiss all such accounts as being no more than the mental meandering of the insane. Others too have written of enlightenment. The Japanese Master Kosen Imakita described his own experience:

One night as I sat absorbed in meditation I suddenly fell into a strange state. It was as if I were dead and everything had been totally cut off. There was no longer any before or after and both the object of my meditation and my Self had disappeared. The only remaining feeling was that my innermost Self was completely filled by and at one with everything above, below and around me.

An infinite light shone within me. After a while I came back to myself like one risen from the dead. Seeing, hearing, movement and thoughts all seemed completely transformed from what they had previously been.[6]

We can see the same themes of transformation in the words of the song sung by the Lady Yeshe Tsogel:

My birth was low but my merit great;
Now my body has been transfigured
And ordinary vision has permanently vanished;
The *samadi* in which all is illusion has arisen,
And I control the five elements.
Now my speech has become a *mantra*
And useless vacant gossip is a thing of the past;
The *vajra*-like *samadhi* has arisen,
And intuitively I know and use the modes of *sutra* and *tantra*
Now my mind has become Buddha
And my ordinary thoughts have vanished into empty space;
The *samadhi* of a bodhisattva has arisen.[7]

Preparing for enlightenment

We should never limit the experience of enlightenment through establishing a prescriptive model. Each breakthrough is totally unique with its own momentum and dynamics. Those best qualified to share the moment of revelation have also been those most reluctant to discuss it; personal description would be converted into the bedrock of hard truth by the unenlightened. There remain relatively few accounts to which we can turn as reference points. This is intentional. Do not look to history for a model, just believe that it can happen for you if that is what you want. Though we cannot limit the nature of the experience in any way, we can say that such a dramatic breakthrough requires preparation if we are not to be totally swept away by the enormity of the moment itself. Any graduated path permits an organic movement of transition from one state to another until the whole being is ready. In this way enlightenment falls as easily as a ripe fruit. Buddhism has placed much emphasis on the development of particular qualities of being. Equanimity, benefiting others, dependence on others, cherishing others and exchanging self for others, all serve to prepare the mind for the realization that the perceived others and the self are one and the same. The path in Buddhism traditionally begins with the affirmation of renunciation. Buddhist renunciation has taken on a particular flavour, which may not be universally applicable but it is clear, if we are to move towards the spiritual witness, that we need to willingly renounce the wants of the automaton.

Such preparation serves to affirm the utterly human nature of the enlightenment experience. This breakthrough does not create strange, alienated people but wholly, normal and full human beings. When someone asked the Dalai Lama, 'How can an ordinary person know you are a living Buddha?', he replied, 'A Buddha is someone who is kind to everyone. A Buddha is not someone who behaves extraordinarily, who has supernatural powers or who is lofty.'

The Buddha within

> I salute the Buddha within you. You may not be aware of it, you may not have ever dreamed about it – that you are a Buddha, that nobody can be anything else, that buddhahood is the very essential core of your being, that it is not something to happen in the future, that it has happened already.
>
> Osho, *The Heart Sutra*

When Buddhists meet, greetings are exchanged, the palms are held together like a lotus flower, there is a mindful bow, a moment's inbreath and the silent mutual repetition of the words, 'a lotus for you Buddha to be'. In this beautiful encounter we find a profound acknowledgement; the seeds of awakening are present and Buddha is present in the other. How we see ourselves is crucial. Our self-image is vital to the person we take ourselves to be. Low self-esteem breeds a sense of unworthiness. High self-esteem brings self-worth. What self-estimation can surpass the divine? Identifying ourselves with the highest and the eternal is not presumptuous but a deep spiritual affirmation. When we see sacred images as being external models we place an unbreachable gap between the human and the divine. When the Buddha is on a pedestal, it becomes impossible to live like a Buddha. When the Christ is worshipped only from afar, it becomes impossible to realize the Christ within. In Tantric Buddhism the quality of Divine Pride is specifically developed. This is quite unlike the pride that afflicts, but it is a statement of total identification with the indestructible. We have been searching for the self on our quest. We will not find it in diminished definitions. We should not settle for the common-sense view, for common sense takes us nowhere. Let us look to multi-dimensional definitions, which offer unlimited possibilities. Geshe Rabten reminds us that the self has two modes of being: a conventional mode and an ultimate mode. If we admit the limitations of our conventional expressions, let us also look towards the unlimited possibilities of an ultimate reality. Let us see in it the best: love, wisdom and compassion. Let us name it in a way that inspires us. Let us hear the words of Osho again: 'Let it be there in your heart that you are a Buddha. I know it may look presumptuous, it may look very hypothetical; you cannot trust it totally. That is natural. I understand it, let it be there but as a seed.'[8] The exoteric path of religion upholds its own codes and directs us towards its founders as teachers and exemplars. The esoteric spiritual path takes us towards a total identification of being.

EXERCISE 12.2 THE DIVINE SEED

How do you see yourself? As we grow up, family and friends apply many labels. Some are supportive, others are destructive. Instead of accepting the labels of others, choose your own and let them affirm the highest that you imagine. Take a specific divine image from a tradition you feel in harmony with. If possible have a picture or other representation in front of you. Meditate on everything it stands for. Visualize the image very clearly in your own mind, then transfer it to the heart centre. Allow the image to become smaller and smaller until it resembles a tiny seed of light. Give it a space in your heart and the seed will take root.

The central mystery

The feeling of awe and the sense of wonder arise from the recognition the deep mystery that surrounds us everywhere, and this feeling deepens as our knowledge grows.

Lama Govinda, *Creative Meditation*

Who can doubt that the fullness of life remains a mystery to us? It is beyond our comprehension. Yet we can recognize the mystery itself. We do not have to understand it, explain it, or justify it. It simply is. The vastness of creation cannot be comprehended, yet the human heart urges us to make our connection with it. Stars unseen, planets unknown and galaxies unnamed beckon us. Black holes and white holes dwarf our understanding. Cosmic life outstrips our measure. Serious scientists now put forward explanations that are infinitely more strange than any metaphysical speculation, such as dark matter and a multiverse containing many parallel universes! Surely this resembles the stuff of fantasy. Contemporary discoveries in science deepen our sense of wonder. Quantum physics takes us into a realm that is barely recognizable to common sense:

> A tree, a table, a cloud, a stone – all are resolved by twentieth-century sciences into one similarly constituted thing: a congeries of whirling particle-waves obeying the laws of quantum physics. That is, all the objects we observe are three-dimensional images formed of standing and moving waves by electromagnetic and nuclear processes.[9]

This view of reality is very close to the Buddhist axiom, 'Emptiness is form, form is emptiness.' The enlightenment experience may even be a glimpse into this level of reality, which is the world of behind the world. Multi-level consciousness enables us to hold more than one view of the world simultaneously.

The quantum paradigm may be recent but earlier mystical models also express a holographic view of creation. In the *Avatamsaka Sutra*, we find the jewelled net of Indra. In each knot there is a jewel and each jewel reflects all others. In the same way each object in the world is not merely itself but involves every other object and in fact is everything else. In every particle of dust there are present Buddhas without number. We do not act in the light of this metaphor. We do not act in the light of interconnectedness. We still act in the light of the Newtonian model, which describes a world of solid objects and empty space. Yet the quantum model is the new paradigm. Its ramifications will continue to alter the view of ourselves and reality: 'The full meaning of quantum theory is still in the stage of being born. In my opinion, the quantum principle involves mind in an essential way.'[10] Albert Einstein, the founder of quantum physics, himself expressed his own awe:

> The most beautiful thing we can experience is the mysterious. It is the source of all true art and science. He to whom this emotion is a stranger, who can no longer pause to wonder and stand wrapped in awe, is as good as dead; his eyes are closed.

Experience indicates that we are unable to ignore the greater reality around us. Which civilization has ever ignored the mysteries of time and space and the mysteries of being and becoming? In response to the unreachable, we reach out through myth, fantasy, story and the world of the imagination. We can only recognize the great mystery that lies at the heart of existence. Knowledge itself takes us no nearer; the more we understand the less we understand. Every new discovery reveals a new puzzle.

Meditation has its place in this radical new view. If mind has some intrinsic role to play in the appearance of reality then we would do well to address the nature of mind as the ancient traditions have always done. Through meditation, which is nothing less than the transformation of consciousness, we can find a place in the greater whole. The great paradox of being is resolved in the human heart when we know where we belong. D.T. Suzuki, the much-acclaimed Zen teacher, speaks of meditation:

> [It] opens the mind of man to the greatest mystery that takes place daily and hourly; it widens the heart so that it may feel the eternity of time and the infinity of space in every throb; it gives us a life within the world as if we were moving about in paradise; and all these spiritual deeds take place without any refuge to doctrine, but by the simple and direct holding fast to the truth which dwells in our innermost being.[11]

The mystery at the heart of creation finds its parallel in mythic and universal symbolism. The sacred vessel easily pre-dates the grail of the Arthurian legends. It is the cauldron of rebirth, the bestower of plenty and the prize of the quest. It is the mystery which resides simultaneously in the depths of the human heart and the centre of creation.

EXERCISE 12.3 THE GRAIL OF BEING AND BECOMING

Find yourself in a sacred space of your own choosing, whether temple, grove or shrine. Build this place to your own specifications. Decorate the scene with sacred symbols of your own choosing. If no symbols come to mind, just include a lighted candle. Take a seat here and enter a deep state of meditation. As you sit, you hear the sound of women's voices singing some way off. As you wait their singing grows nearer. Now you realize that the sounds are close by. You hear the rustle of skirts and the step of feet. You instinctively stand. You are joined in your sacred place by a procession of women who walk at a stately pace in pairs. The procession is led by a single woman, who carries a veiled chalice. The grail bearer halts as the procession forms a circle within the sacred space. The singing stops as all reach their places. There is a deep and profound silence. The grail bearer lifts the chalice aloft. As you watch it seems to you that the grail begins to radiate a soft luminescence even though it remains veiled; light emanates from within and its light seems palpable. The light from the grail takes shape as tiny individual flames flicker and dance in the sacred space. As you watch, a flame alights over the head of all those present. As you observe others you see that the flame is disappearing into the top of your head and you realize that others can see this happening to you. You make yourself open to the entrance of the Light of the grail. You enter deeper meditation. Time passes and the external lights have faded, but all the faces seem to glow with an inner radiance. The members of the procession stand and depart quietly and in peace. You remain alone until you wish to close the meditation. When you are ready to depart allow the images to fade.

13 bodymind – the new frontier

In this chapter you will learn:
- more about the unity of mind and body
- more about the latest research into meditation
- more about the life choices you can make.

The physical brain

> The fabric of the brain has been discovered within the last 150 years.
>
> *The Oxford Companion to the Mind*

Exploration and discovery never cease; new frontiers always beckon. Each breakthrough changes the view we hold of ourselves and the world in which we live; prevailing certainties invariably give way to a new paradigm. The Victorians looked at the shape of the head to explain how the mind worked; we are able to watch the brain at work, phrenology has given way to neuroscience. We now stand at the dawning of a new understanding of mind, brain and body: the bodymind is the new frontier.

The brain is a remarkable physical organ, a living computer which directs thoughts, memories, behaviours and moods. It co-ordinates the five senses, constantly reviewing all stimuli from the internal organs and the surface of the body, making minute and precise adjustments continuously.

Everything we associate with human culture – values, beliefs, social organization, artistic creativity and scientific understanding – has its roots in our ability to process and reorder the external world through the mediation of the brain; no computer can match its capabilities. Even though the human brain can be dissected, measured, observed, recorded and analysed, consciousness that arises from the activity of the brain remains invisible and elusive, here is the ultimate conundrum.

At its simplest, the brain can be described as being composed of three main areas: the cerebrum, the brain stem and the cerebellum. The most recently evolved cerebral cortex, the surface of the cerebrum, has been called, 'the mother of invention and father of abstract thought'. Commonly called grey matter, its folds and ridges hold about 10 billion neurons with about 50 trillion synapses; it is here that the uniquely human qualities of perception, imagination, thought, judgment and decision making are processed. Beneath, a second layer of white matter serves to create interconnections with other parts of the central nervous system. A deep furrow divides the cerebrum into two halves that remain connected by the nerve fibres of the corpus callosum, even though each hemisphere processes its own specific and often separate functions. The two hemispheres of the cerebral cortex are further divided into four distinct lobes: frontal, parietal, occipital and temporal. The frontal lobes are concerned with reasoning, planning, parts of speech and voluntary movement, personality, emotions and intelligence. The parietal lobes interpret sensory information from the body and control body movement and spatial awareness. The occipital lobes process and interpret vision, enable people to form visual memories and integrate visual and spatial perceptions. The temporal lobes generate memory and emotions, comprehend sounds and images, and enable the process of recognition. The brain stem connects the cerebrum with the spinal cord and automatically regulates critical body functions, such as breathing, swallowing, blood pressure and heartbeat, also serving to adjust posture. The cerebellum stores memories of practised movements, enabling the development of highly specialized skills seen in dance, sport and feats of balance. Describing the bare physical anatomy of the brain cannot answer the greatest mystery of our human nature – where are we to be found as unique individuals in the neural architecture of electrical pulse and synapse?

The chemical brain

Absolutely anyone – regardless of time, mood or previous experience – can create a sense of well-being and build a lasting foundation for all other forms of personal development. Whenever you want – in the midst of family pressure, anxious colleagues, an urgent crisis or seemingly unbearable stress – you can trigger the production of your endorphins, feel better and once again sense the good things of life.

William Bloom, *The Endorphin Effect*

The electrical activity of the brain cannot be separated from its partnership with the brain's chemical processes. The brain produces more than 50 identified active drugs, and chemical reactions take place every second, creating a finely orchestrated interplay that directly affects mood, behaviour and health. Specific changes in brain chemistry produce specific changes in behaviour. Breakthroughs in scientific and medical understanding are both exciting and important as new possibilities and applications take shape. The discovery of the endorphin marks another frontier in our understanding of the bodymind.

As with so many discoveries, endorphins were discovered almost incidentally by scientists researching drug addiction.

Investigating why the human brain contained receptors for chemicals produced by a plant, the opiate producing poppy, it was discovered that the brain produces its own neurochemicals that share the same receptors. Termed 'endogenous morphine', a new term entered chemical vocabulary, the endorphin – morphine produced within the body itself. Produced by the pituitary gland and the hypothalamus, the body's own morphine, the endorphin, can produce analgesia and a sense of well-being. Four distinct groups of endorphins have been identified so far: alpha, beta, gamma and sigma. Probably evolved through the millennia of human evolution, this natural body chemistry is related to the fight or flight syndrome and our ability to endure pain and trauma.

It is currently believed that endorphins produce four key effects on the bodymind: enhancing the immune system, relieving pain, reducing stress and postponing the ageing process. In other words, endorphins are good for you. Originally, it was thought that endorphin production was restricted to the brain, but in the 1980s it was discovered that they were secreted throughout the whole system, once again affirming the unity of mind and body. Endorphins can be produced at any location in the body to flow through the whole system like waves in an ocean; the body's nervous system, immune system and endocrine system are all intimately interlinked. This is a powerful affirmation of holism. The neuroscientist Candice Pert, who was involved in the original research into opiates, stakes a claim for the integrated body/mind. In her book, *Molecules of Emotion*, she states:

> The point I am making is that your brain is extremely well integrated with the rest of your body at a molecular level, so much so that the term mobile brain is an apt description of the psychosomatic network through which intelligent information travels from one system to another. Every one of the zones, or systems, of the network – the neural, the hormonal, the gastrointestinal, and the immune – is set up to communicate with one another, via peptides and messenger-specific peptide receptors. Every second, a massive information exchange is happening in your body. Imagine each of these messenger systems possessing a specific tone, humming a signature tune, rising and falling, waxing and waning, binding and unbinding, and if we could hear this body music with our ears, then the sum of these sounds would be the music that we call the emotions.

Here is a revolutionary perspective: 'the mobile brain' – a seed thought worthy of meditation. Pert suggests life enhancing strategies to maximize the endorphin effect: 'becoming conscious, daily relaxation, enjoyable exercise, "pointless" recreational activities, tapping into our dreams, guiltless goofing off, experiencing pleasure in little things, public and private displays of affection, sex without guilt, greater laughter and additional sources of merriment.' Endorphins are naturally produced by a wide range of emotional, mental and physical triggers including exercise, laughter, deep breathing, meditation, massage, music, and most subtly by our states of mind. Studies have shown that chronic stress, anger and depression cause the body to manufacture chemicals that inhibit the healing process and shorten life expectancy; euphoria protects us from stress, illness and premature death. So chose euphoria, choose endorphin!

The emotional brain

> The revolution we call mind-body medicine was based on this simple discovery: wherever a thought goes, a chemical goes with it.

> Deepak Chopra, *Holistic Revolution – The Essential New Age Reader*

The physical brain reflects a long evolutionary development. Our rational thought processes belong to the neocortex, the newest area of the brain, but rationality is a relatively young acquisition; reflection before action remains a finely balanced ability that can be swamped by emotional triggers from older instinctual processes within the brain. It was the neurophysiologist Paul MacLean who made a significant contribution to our understanding of the brain through his triune theory of the brain.[1] This states that we posses three brains – biological computers – each connected to the other two while independently possessing unique characteristics, specialized intelligence, subjectivity, temporal and spatial awareness and memory. Only in human beings and higher mammals do these three brains co-exist: the neocortex or the neo-mammalian brain, the limbic or paleo-mammalian system, and the reptilian brainstem and cerebellum, each representing an evolutionary layer. The limbic system as defined by MacLean has proven to be more complex and less unified, but in principle it is accepted that our most basic instinctive survival drives are patterned within his biological circuitry and most especially centred upon the amygdala.[2]

Given certain circumstances, this small almond-shaped neuro-structure has the power to completely disrupt thinking. Responding to both unconscious and conscious perceptions, nonverbal signs of anger or fear, the amygdala releases hormones into the bloodstream to produce physical reactions such as sweaty palms, tense-mouth display and a range of defensive postures including the complete body freeze. This is our instinctive alarm button hot wired for survival. It served our ancestors well but contemporary life does not pose the same life threatening challenges on a daily basis. However, once aroused, the instinctive response can hijack rationality and precipitate acts of extreme passion, anger and violence. Using Functional Magnetic Resonance Imaging (MRI), researchers have watched the hot emotionally charged centres of the brain interfere with the cooler cognitive processes. The amygdala is also associated with the forming and storing of emotional memories, another survival mechanism. Conditions where emotional memories assume disproportionate importance, such as anxiety, depression, phobia and even post-traumatic stress disorder, are suspected of being linked to abnormal functioning of the amygdala. Understanding the mechanisms through which the amygdala functions may assist to empower those strategies, whether educational, psychological or spiritual, that serve to retain control with the neocortex, the thinking brain. The amygdyla is highly sensitized: synchronized to changes in the heart beat, attuned to external nonverbalized threats, connected to each hemisphere, this inner alarm system misses no opportunity to react. Yet we do not live by survival alone, and it is possible to exercise the control offered through the neocortex to modify an emotional response rather than being swept away on a hormonal tide. When this part of the brain is stimulated with a mild electrical current, various emotions – fear, joy, rage and pleasure – are produced. Simply knowing that the amygdala has the power to produce what we have come to call our emotions reveals the powerful truth that such feelings are physical brain processes. The amygdala has vast interconnections with the neocortex. Throughout the mammal kingdom, including humans, the brain is wired so that the connecting pathways from the amygdala to the cortex overshadow the pathways from the cortex to the amygdala. In other words, the connections to the thinking brain are stronger and more numerous than those from the thinking system to the emotional systems. This means that thoughts can easily trigger emotions by activating the amygdala, but thoughts do not have the same power to turn off the emotions by deactivating the amygdala. The limbic circuitry and its attendant implications can, however, be accorded a proper place and be kept in proportioned perspective by educating the emotions.

Daniel Goleman is one among a new breed of commentators: highly qualified in Western psychology, while simultaneously in dialogue with Eastern Buddhist experience. His several works have introduced a Western audience to a new concept, namely Emotional Intelligence (EQ). Strategies for fostering EQ may appear new to the institutions now implementing such programmes with gusto, but in truth, the nuts and bolts of EQ are familiar to all spiritual practitioners. The age old meditative techniques – self-awareness, mindfulness, detached self-witnessing, conscious breathing, practical ways of approaching the emotions and the mind, the principles of moral responsibility and the development of compassion – have become the building blocks of a Western newly discovered EQ and its twin Spiritual Intelligence (SQ). It seems ironic that the American business community has quickly seen the dividend to be made from implementing EQ, whereas the education community has been somewhat slower to act. Nevertheless, the development of self-awareness, emotional balance, motivation and empathy has been given a rightful place where good relationships matter.

EQ provides the antidote to the impulsive action spurred by the alarm system. A moment of conscious detachment enables us to stop, reflect and reason, thereby putting a brake on the super highway between the amygdala and frontal lobe. Communication between the emotional and the reasoning brain is maintained via the neurotransmitter serotonin. Optimum levels permit healthy, normal communication but anger especially burns up serotonin very quickly. Is it merely coincidental that according to Buddhism anger is among the root delusions? Optimal levels of serotonin also bring increased self-confidence, self-control and calmness of mind. Optimal levels are maintained by holding a positive mental attitude to all life experiences; it is impossible not to be reminded of the Buddhist view: equanimity in all things. Meditative traditions offer a wisdom gained over centuries – who would not wish to listen and benefit?

The electrical brain

How does the brain work – what does it actually do? These questions have fascinated and challenged countless human beings over many centuries. At last, we now have the expertise to tackle what might arguably be regarded as the final frontier in human understanding.

Susan Greenfield, *The Human Brain*

The brain is electrochemical in nature. In this amazing wonderland, the neuron conducts a tiny electrical gradient across individual cell membranes signalling to other neurones or muscle tissue. Magnified billions of times, this transaction permits every action and thought that we take. The electrical nature of the brain was first realized towards the end of the nineteenth century, but the invention of the EEG (electroencephalogram) recorder in 1929 permitted the invisible electrical landscape of the brain to become visible. Early researchers were limited by the slow visual interpretation of the raw data. It was not until the mid-1960s that computer analysis permitted EEG data to be separated into various frequency bands called Alpha, Beta, Delta and Theta. This new understanding may well have contributed to the booming interest in the therapeutic possibilities of the Alpha state that appeared then. Several decades later, the EEG has been supplemented by Functional MRI and Positron Emission Tomography (PET). Historically, researchers have recognized four major brain rhythms although without precise agreement on the exact frequency ranges for each type. Loosely, the range commences with the Delta rhythm from 0.1 to 4 Hz, moves into the Theta frequency from 4 to 8 Hz, reaches the Alpha state from 8 to 13 Hz and continues with the Beta rhythm from 13 Hz and beyond. However, technical refinements have extended the observable range in both directions, recording extremely slow frequencies at less than 0.5 Hz and much faster frequencies that resonate at 40 Hz and above. Some researchers claim to have noted even higher frequencies close to 100 Hz, although this remains unexplored territory. The newly recognized frequency beyond the Beta range is creating much interest. Called Gamma, although some researchers prefer it to be known as High Beta, it is thought to be the signature of much deeper activity at neurone level. The Gamma frequency is essential to higher mental activity, perception and states of self-awareness, and high levels of insight and information processing. Some studies have linked the Gamma range to ESP (extrasensory perception), heightened insight, and even OBEs (out of body experiences).

Brain wave frequency correlates to mental states or types of activity. The Delta frequency is associated with the very young and is seen in deep sleep. The Theta frequency is associated with drowsiness, childhood and adolescence. Theta waves can be seen during states such as trances, hypnosis, deep day dreams, lucid dreaming, light sleep and the preconscious state just upon waking, and just before falling asleep. The Alpha frequency is characteristic of a relaxed but alert state of consciousness best detected with the eyes closed. Low amplitude Beta with multiple and varying frequencies is often associated with active, busy or anxious thinking and active concentration. High amplitude Beta can be related to anxious alertness. Nonetheless, Gamma activity seems to correlate with some unique functions. It seems to occur when various chemical messengers enable efficient communication across large swathes of brain tissue, most probably through the synchronized firing of entire banks of neurons. Recent studies have shown that new insights occur when frequencies suddenly shift from 20 to 40 Hz. This 40 Hz rhythm seems to be vital to the process of synthesis, binding separate data into a single experience. For instance, object, colour, size and texture are all processed by different parts of the brain, but the Gamma frequency unifies this diverse information into a single experience. No other brain frequency is involved in this process. Since research has already shown that sufferers from schizophrenia lack this unifying rhythm, the Gamma wave might even be described as the neurological signature of holism. Is it possible that the Gamma wave is related to a sense of oneness and loss of self commonly reported in deep meditative states? Recently, the Gamma signature has become the object of intense scientific interest; its documented appearance in a much reported project with Tibetan monks has caused something of a stir.

Meditation and neuroscience

What we found is that the trained mind, or brain, is physically different from the untrained one.

Richard Davidson

Meditation is ancient, neuroscience is contemporary. Unexpectedly, the two fields are now to be found in unusual liason; both share common territory in the abiding quest to understand mind, brain and consciousness. This entirely new and recent possibility renders the invisible visible as meditative practice can be seen impacting into the neural network. The technical and the spiritual together are now making it possible to observe the meditative mind at work. The correlation between mental activity and brainwave patterns has been known since the 1960s. This key finding did much to fuel a cultural revolution centred on the spiritualization of values along with the introduction of practical meditative principles such as positive affirmation, visualization, relaxation and techniques for mindfulness. Now, further research has refined the original conception and moved the ensuing debate to a new plateau: biofeedback has moved into neurofeedback. Tibetan Buddhist monks have become key figures in this current chapter whereas the early subjects involved in laboratory studies were most often Indian yogis or gurus. Professor Richard Davidson, from the University of Wisconsin-Madison, currently proposes that meditative practice literally alters brain structure. Where the West has excelled in the technology of objective empiricism, the East has refined a technology of subjective experience. Together, these two components open up the extraordinary possibility of peering into the mind-brain interface. Western science and philosophy have long wrestled with a central debate: whether the mind is created by the brain, whether consciousness itself might be reduced to neural activity; Buddhism proposes a model that places mind quite beyond brain. This rich cross-fertilization must surely benefit us all. At a time when many varied meditative techniques are being used as the basis for new Western therapeutic approaches, it is both timely and beneficial that neuroscience can inform the debate. New technology permits an objective assessment of change, meditation practices may be seen to promote beneficial changes in the brain.

On Saturday 12 November 2005, His Holiness, the Dalai Lama, gave the inaugural lecture to the prestigious Society for Neuroscience on The Neuroscience of Meditation. As co-founder of the Mind and Life Institute, the Dalai Lama has long sought to promote the dialogue between science and Buddhism.[3] Richard Davidson also bridges the scientific and the spiritual. Having spent much time in India on meditation retreat, he now directs the Waisman Laboratory for Brain Imaging and Behaviour. In his recent and much reported research, he compared brain activity in volunteer novice meditators with that of highly experienced Buddhist monks. Using magnetic resonance imaging, the researchers were able to pinpoint the brain regions made active during the particular meditation that involved the generation of loving kindness and compassion. Where the novice meditators showed a slight increase in Gamma activity, the experienced meditators showed Gamma waves that were 30 times as strong and, according to Davidson, 'of a sort that has never been reported before in the neuroscience literature'. Neural activity was predominant in the left prefrontal cortex, the seat of positive emotions such as happiness. The regions responsible for planned movement were also highly activated, as if the monks were getting ready to act. In Buddhism there can be no compassion without action, this is the concept of Karuna, devoted action to alleviate suffering.

Meditation may appear to be a passive process, but in fact it is uniquely dynamic, creating greater levels of consciousness along with both short- and long-term neural change. Functional MRI has revolutionized brain research, making it possible to map changes in the brain. At the Laboratory for Affective Neuroscience and the W.M. Keck Laboratory for Functional Brain Imaging and Behaviour where Buddhist meditation meets Western technology, the old notion of neuroplasticity has been reinvigorated. The term refers to the brain's ability to change its structure and function. Previously thought to be a characteristic only of the very young, it is now clear that the brain has the capacity to develop new neural connections throughout life. Clearly the neuroplasticity of the brain permits recovery from injury and disease, however, it now seems that this ability also responds to internal mentally generated signals. Davidson and his team have correlated emotional states and brain activity, finding that states of happiness, enthusiasm and joy show up as increased activity on the left side near the front of the cortex, while states of anxiety and sadness show as increased activity on the right. This pattern appears in infants as young as 10 months, in toddlers, teens and adults. Researchers at Wisconsin University have been able to render the mental experiences of meditation into the scientific vocabulary of high-frequency Gamma waves and brain co-ordination but, translated into everyday language, this is the impact of mind upon matter. In Davidson's words:

> What we found is that the longtime practitioners showed brain activation on a scale we have never seen before. Their mental practice has an effect on the brain in the same way golf or tennis practice enhances performance. It demonstrates, that the brain is capable of being trained and physically modified in ways few people can imagine.

The brain, like the rest of the body, can be altered intentionally.

A new area of research and development is already opening, namely the interface of brain power and technology. Once only a fiction from the pen of Arthur C. Clarke, the brain computer interface is now a reality, translating brainwaves into computer instruction. In Tokyo, the Japanese automaker, Honda, is developing a brain-machine interface. Although this technology is still in its infancy, the first step has been taken. Brain signals detected by an MRI scanner have been used to control the simple movements of a robotic hand. In the US, the Wadsworth centre, together with Cambridge Consultants in the UK, has also produced a brain computer interface (BCI). Worn as a cap, the BCI system translates brainwaves into computer commands without the need for electrodes. The possibilities for enabling people with spinal cord or other disabling injuries are clear, but this neuro-technology may in time produce amazing developments. Honda, in conjunction with Computational Neuroscience Laboratories, envisages that new technology might in time replace keyboards or cell phones. It is impossible to say where this interface might lead; this is the Age of Aquarius, symbolic of mind, and its co-ruler is Uranus, representing technical innovation – the marriage of mind and machine is already under way.

The whole life – the happy life

Relax, rejuvenate, energize. Most of all enjoy *being* in the beautiful, healthy body that you have helped create for yourself, now and for the rest of your life.

Susan Levy and Carol Lehr, *Your Body Can Talk*

The holistic life is the whole life, and it can be the happy life. Recognizing the interplay of mind and body, thought and feeling, heart and soul is to acknowledge the essential unity of being.

The Western mind seems to have come to this realization only lately, whereas the older meditative mystical traditions have taken this relationship to be self-evident. The West, almost alone, discarded this sense of wholeness and only now, after centuries of estrangement, does it feel obliged to apply the full panoply of scientific weight so that it might not just believe but also understand. When the West's view of the bodymind undergoes sufficient revision, then it will have crossed the barrier between separation and holism. The West most often adopts practical goals; improved health and stress management means less absence at work, greater productivity and less burden on the health services. Such pragmatic goals serve the individual too. This practical approach has already served to take meditation practice out from the temple or ashram and place it in the workplace, the community centre, even in the school. Such new initiatives continue to spread as a more holistic philosophy enters the worlds of business, health and education, worlds that measure success not by personal subjective experience but by hard and fast criteria of goal orientated targets. The divide between the spiritual and the secular, once seen as a chasm, is being bridged by individuals, institutions and organizations.

Empirical evidence has discovered what spiritual tradition has always known, namely that a dynamic correlation exists between mind and body. The coming together of science and mysticism creates a fascinating union between the East and West. The holistic health revolution is still unfolding, the bodymind frontier is revealing a new realm of extraordinary interaction and marvellous complexity. Holism, the inner secret of all sacred traditions, is here to stay, dressed in a new form for the twenty-first century – the bodymind.

Ajna Sanskrit title for the brow chakra.

Anahata Sanskrit name for the heart chakra.

Arhat The liberated state in Hinayana Buddhism, a 'worthy one'.

Asanas A posture, third of the Eight Limbs of Yoga.

Atman The universal consciousness.

Avidya Lack of wisdom.

ayama Ascension, expansion and extension.

Bardo To enter incarnation at birth.

Bodhicitta Awakening mind.

Bodhi mind The awakened mind.

Bodhisattva One who seeks liberation for the sake of others.

Buddha Awakened mind.

chakra A psychic or spiritual centre, a wheel of living energy.

Chin mudra A seal, a way of holding the hands during meditation.

Citta Consciousness.

Cosmic Consciousness The conscious realization of the whole.

Devekut The Judaic term for the enlightened state.

dharma The law, the teachings.

Dharana Concentration, attention focusing on the sixth of the eight aspects of Yoga.

Dhikr A Sufi practice, remembering the name of God.

Dhyana Meditation, reflection, observation of the seventh of the eight aspects of Yoga.

Dokusan The daily interview with the Zen teacher.

Gnosis Direct knowing.

Gunas The three qualities of Nature.

Hinayana The Lesser Vehicle, the Buddhist spiritual path for self-liberation.

Jnana mudra   A seal, a way of holding the hands in meditation.
Kabbalah   The Jewish mystical tradition.
Karuna   Compassion.
kavvanah   Intentionality, mental concentration.
Koan   A Zen meditation in the form of a paradox.
mahat   Universal consciousness.
Mahayana   The Greater Vehicle, the Buddhist spiritual path for the liberation of all.
Mandala   A meditation represented in circular form.
manipura   The Sanskrit name for the solar plexus chakra.
mantra   Sounded word or phrase.
Moksha   The Hindu term for liberation.
Mujodo no taigeu   The Zen term for the enlightened state.
Muladhara   The Sanskrit name for the base chakra.
nirvana   The cessation of sufferings and desires.
Niyama   The five ethical observances, second of the Eight Limbs of Yoga.
Otz Chiim   The Tree of Life.
Padma   A lotus.
prana   The universal life force.
pranayama   Breath control.
Pratyhara   Sense withdrawal.
Sahasrara   The Sankrit name for the crown chakra.
Samsara   The cycle of being, incarnation after incarnation.
Sangha   The spiritual community.
Sepher Yetzirah   The Book of Formations, mystical Judaic text.
Sphira, Sephroth   The Divine Emanations.
Shri Yantra   The yantra of creation composed of nine interpenetrating triangles.
Shunyata   Spaciousness, openness.
svayambhu   An evolved soul who incarnates in order to help humanity.
Svadisthana   The Sanksrit name for the sacral chakra.
Teisho   The Zen ceremonial commentary delivered to elucidate a koan.
Theravada   The school of Buddhism widespread in Southeast Asia and Sri Lanka.
Vidya   Wisdom.
Vipassana   Penetrative insight.
Vishnu Granthi   The knot of living energy in the heart chakra.
Vishuddi   The Sanskrit name for the throat chakra.
yantra   A meditation in geometric form.
Zazen   Sitting meditation.
Zohar   The basic text of Jewish mysticism.

notes

Preface
1 Gray, *Practical Miracles*, p. 5
2 Gray, *Practical Miracles*, p. 17
3 Marshall and Zohar, *Spiritual Intelligence*, p. 9
4 Marshall and Zohar, *Spiritual Intelligence*, p. 14
5 Marshall and Zohar, *Spiritual Intelligence*, p. 4
6 Marshall and Zohar, *Spiritual Intelligence*, p. 296

Chapter 01
1 Rabten, *Treasury of Dharma*, 1988, p. 122
2 Sogyal Rinpoche, *Meditation*, 1994, p. 89.

Chapter 02
1 Wilbur *et al.*, *Transformations in Consciousness*, 1991,
  p. 27
2 D. Brown and J. Engler, 'The stages of mindfulness
  meditation: a validation study', *Transpersonal
  Psychology*, 1980, 12, 2, pp. 143–92
3 Wilbur *et al.*, *Transformations*, p. 197
4 Rabten, *Dharma*, p. 21
5 Govinda, *Creative Meditation*, 1977, p. 17
6 Sogyal Rinpoche, *Meditation*, p. 84

Chapter 03
1 Lucis Trust, *The Science of Meditation*, p. 5
2 Osho, *The Everyday Meditator*, 1993, p. 56
3 Sheng Yen, *Catching a Feather on a Fan*, p. 37
4 Rabten, *Dharma*, p. 167
5 Nhat Hanh, *Miracle of Mindfulness*, p. 22
6 *Experimenal Meditation Journal of Nervous and Mental
  Diseases*, 1963, p. 136

Chapter 04
1 Fortune, *The Mystical Qabalah*, 1976, p. 18
2 Lawler, *Sacred Geometry*, 1982, p. 108

Chapter 05
1 Schwaller de Lubicz, *The Opening of the Way*, 1979, p. 60
2 Nhat Hanh, *The Sun My Heart*, 1988, p. 66
3 Ibid, p. 72
4 Lucis Trust, *Science of Meditation*, p. 5
5 Rabten, *Dharma*, p. 175
6 Osho, *The Heart Sutra*, 1994, p. 26
7 Govinda, *Creative Meditation*, p. 143

Chapter 06
1 Lancaster, *Mind, Brain and Human Potential*, 1991, p. 101
2 Priestly, J.B., *Man and Time*, p. 290
3 Govinda, *Creative Meditation*, p. 151
4 Lewis, C.S., *Voyage of the Dawn Treader*, p. 12
5 Govinda, *Creative Meditation*, p. 43
6 Skolimowski, *EcoYoga*, 1994, p. 122
7 Govinda, *Creative Meditation*, p. 41
8 Lancaster, *Human Potential*, p. 85
9 *New Scientist*, no. 2074
10 Lancaster, *Human Potential*, p. 114
11 Tucci, *Theory and Practice of the Mandala*, 1969, p. 25
12 Jung, *Memories, Dreams and Reflections*, 1973, p. 221

Chapter 07
1 Batchelor, *Walking on Lotus Flowers*, 1996, p. 4
2 Skolimowski, *EcoYoga*, p. 153
3 Ibid, p. 22
4 Extracts from Herrigel, *Zen in the Art of Archery*, 1985, as follows:
'artless art', p. 18
'spiritual exercises', p. 14
'It is necessary', p. 16
'The shot will only', p. 44
'I draw the bow', p. 46
'The more obstinately.', p. 46
'It shot', p. 74
'Put the thought', p. 79
'Your arrows do not', p. 77
'I must warn you', p. 90
'presence of heart', p. 96

'egoless and purposeless', p. 96
'when the heart ', p. 101
5 Osho, *Everyday Meditator*, p. 197

Chapter 08
1 Nhat Hanh, *The Sun My Heart*, p. 64,
2 Govinda, *Creative Meditation*, p. 15
3 Nhat Hanh, *The Sun My Heart*, p. 18
4 Ibid., p. 19
5 Ibid., p. 14
6 Hoffman, *The Heavenly Ladder*, 1996, p. 51
7 Batchelor, *Walking on Lotus Flowers*, p. 188
8 Kabat-Zinn, *Mindfulness Meditation for Everyday Life*, 1994, p. 202
9 Govinda, *Creative Meditation*, p. 270
10 Kabat-Zinn, *Mindfulness Meditation*, p. 245
11 Hoffman, *The Heavenly Ladder*, p. 74
12 Osho, *Heart Sutra*, p. 68

Chapter 09
1 Enomiya-Lassalle, *The Practice of Zen Meditation*, 1987, p. 22
2 Sogyal Rinpoche, *Meditation*, p. 47
3 Osho, *Heart Sutra*, p. 68

Chapter 10
1 Skolimowski, *EcoYoga*, p. 89
2 Kramer, *Transforming the Inner and Outer Family*, 1995, p. 101
3 Lewis, C.S., *The Magician's Nephew*, Lion, p. 96
4 Segal, *Collision with the Infinite*, 1996, p. 1
5 Govinda, *Creative Meditation*, p. 70
6 Sogyal Rinpoche, *Meditation*, p. 55

Chapter 11
1 Deikman, *The Observing Self*, 1982, p. 142
2 Kramer, *Transforming*, p. 13
3 Ibid., p. 3
4 Ibid., p. 1
5 Schwaller de Lubicz, *Opening the Way*, p. 44
6 Segal, *Collision*, pp. 12, 13, 54, 156, 152
7 Happold, *Mysticism: A Study and an Anthology*, 1963, p. 47
8 Assagioli, *Psychosynthesis*, 1986, p. 197
9 Wilbur, *No Boundaries*, p. 135
10 Osho, *Everday Meditator*, pp. 204–6

11 Zukav, *Dancing Wu Li Masters*, 1980, p. 101
12 Davies, *God and the New Physics*, 1984, p. 111
13 Deikman, *The Observing Self*, p. 62

Chapter 12

1 Hoffman, *Heavenly Ladder*, p. 30
2 Osho, *Heart Sutra*, p. 1
3 Lancaster, *Human Potential*, p. 14
4 Govinda, *Creative Meditation*, p. 210
5 Kapleau, *The Three Pillars of Zen*, 1965, pp. 267–8
6 Enomiya-Lassalle, *Practice of Zen Meditation*, p. 70
7 Dowman, *Sky Dancer*, 1984, p. 87
8 Osho, *Heart Sutra*, p. 4
9 Talbot, *Mysticism and the New Physics*, 1992, p. 47
10 Ibid., p. 2
11 Govinda, *Creative Meditation*, p. 210

Chapter 13

1 See Wikipedia for more information
  (en.wikipedia.org/wiki/Triune_brian)
2 See Wikipedia for more information (as above)
3 See www.mindandlife.org

taking it further

Further reading

Anand, Margot, *The Art of Everyday Ecstasy: The Seven Tantric Keys for Bringing Passion, Spirit and Joy into Every Part of Your Life*, Piatkus, 1998

Angelo, Jack, *Your Healing Power*, Piatkus, 1998

Biddulph, Steve and Sharon, *How Love Works*, Thorson, 2000

Bloom, William, *The Endorphin Effect*, Piatkus, 2001

Bloom, William, *Soulution, The Holistic Manifesto*, Hay House, 2004

Bly, Robert, *The Soul is Here for its own Joy: Sacred Poems from Many Cultures*, The Eco Press, New Jersey, 1995

Brenna, Barbara, *Hand of Light, A Guide to Healing through the Human Energy Field*, Bantam, New York, 1988

Carlson, Robert, *Don't Sweat the Small Stuff at Work*, Hodder & Stoughton, 1998

Carlson, Robert, *Don't Worry Make Money*, Hodder & Stoughton, 1998

Carlson, Robert, *Don't Sweat the Small Stuff*, Hodder & Stoughton, 1997

Castenada, Carlos, *The Teachings of Don Juan*, London, Penguin, 1970

Chopra, Deepak, *The Path to Love: Spiritual Lessons for Creating the Love you Need*, Rider, 1997

Chopra, Deepak, *Ageless Body, Timeless Mind*, Rider, 1993

Cooper, Diana, *The Power of Inner Peace*, Piatkus, 1995

Gill, Edward, *Pure Bliss the Art of Living in Soft Time*, Piatkus, 1999

Goleman, Daniel, *Emotional Intelligence*, Bantam Books, New York, 1996

Goleman, Daniel, *Working with Emotional Intelligence*, Bloomsbury, 1999

Goleman, Daniel, *Destructive Emotions – A Dialogue with the Dalai Lama*, Bloomsbury, 2004

Gray, John, *How to Get What you Want – and Want What you Have*, BCA, 1999

Gray, John, *Mars and Venus Together Forever*, Vermilion, London, 1994

Gray, John, *Men are from Mars Women are from Venus*, HarperCollins, London 1992

Harrison, Eric, *How Meditation Heals*, Piatkus, 2000

Hay, Louise, *Empowering Women: You Can Heal Your Life*, Hodder & Stoughton, London 1998

Holden, Robert, *Shift Happens*, Hodder & Stoughton, 2000

Holden, Robert, *Happiness Now*, Hodder & Stoughton, 2000

Houston, Jean, *The Search for the Beloved*, Tarcher-Putnam, New York, 1987

Houston, Jean, *Life Force: The Psycho-Historical Recovery of the Self*

Houston, Jean, *A Mythic Life: Learning to Live our Greatest Story*, Harper, San Francisco, 1996

Houston, Jean, *A Passion for the Possible*, Thorson, 1998

Dalai Lama, His Holiness the, *Transforming the Mind*, Thorson,

Dalai Lama, His Holiness the, *The Dalai Lama's Little Book of Wisdom*, Rider, 2000

Dalai Lama, His Holiness the and Cutler, Howard, *The Art of Happiness*, Coronet, 1999

Kenton, Leslie, *Journey to Freedom*, HarperCollins, 2000

Kornfield, Jack, *After the Ecstasy the Laundry: How the Heart Grows Wise on the Spiritual Path*, Rider, 2000

Muller, Lawrence G, *Wisdom Roads: Conversations between Masters of Meditation*, Continuum, 2000

Myss, Carolyn, *Why People Don't Heal and How they Can*, Bantam Books, New York, 1998

Myss, Carolyn, *Anatomy of the Spirit*, Bantam, London, 1997

Pert, Candice, *Molecules of Emotion*, Prentice Hall, 1977

Ricard, Matthieu, *Happiness – A Guide to Developing Life's Most Important Skill*, Little, Brown & Company, 2006

Ricard, Matthieu, *The Quantum and the Lotus*, Three Rivers Press, 2004

Spezzani, Chuck, *Whole Heartedness*, Hodder & Stoughton, 2000

Whyte, David, *The Heart Aroused: Poetry and Preservation of the Soul in Corporate America*, Doubleday, 1994

Wise, Anna, *A Guide of Mastering the Power of your Brain Waves*, Tarcher, 2002
Wise, Anna, *High Performance Mind*, Tarcher, 1996
Zukav, Gary, *The Seat of the Soul*, Rider, 2000
Zukav, Gary, *Soul Stories*, Simon & Schuster, 2000

Websites

The Internet provides a fantastic treasury filled with information and possibilities. Let it open your mind to the discovery that the Age of Aquarius has dawned; spirit and matter now walk hand in hand. Questing for the first step of the path is over. Now the choice is simply, 'Which path?', no longer 'Where is the path?' Good luck you will find your own path and the Internet can help you.

Website : www.kabbalah.info/
Name: Glyn Williams Kabbalah Page
Description: Definitions, diagrams, list of resources, discussion, history, meditations, links to sites, activities and organizations.

Website : www.buddhanet.net
Name: Buddhism Information Network.
Description: Meditation techniques, e-books, web links to other sites, events, downloads, hospices, library.

Website : www.iskon.com/
Name: The International Society of Krishna Consciousness.
Description: Official website promoting the well being of society by teaching the science of Krishna consciousness according to *Bhagavad-gita* and other ancient scriptures.

Website : www.zenguide.com/
Name: Zen Guide
Description: Informative and practical outline covering history, concepts, discussion, resources and organizations.

Website : www.wisdom-books.com/
Name: Wisdom Books
Description: An on-line Buddhist book store with an extensive selection.

Website : www.world.std.com/~habib/sufi.html
Name: List of Sufi-related resources on the Internet.
Description: A valuable and thorough resource list of Sufi-related resources.

Website : www.marsvenus.com
Name: John Gray's Universe.
Description: Books, videos, tapes, get practical relationship advice, find a counsellor, bring a spiritual dimension into your day to day relationship.

Website : www.randomhouse.com/features/chopra
Name: Deepak Chopra Official Homepage.
Description: Forum, features, life, works, latests projects.

Website : www.dalailama.com/
Name: His Holiness the Dalai Lama
Description: The life and work of His Holiness Tenzin Gyatso, the 14th Dalai Lama of Tibet, created under the auspices of the Office of Tibet and the Tibetan Government-in-Exile.

Website : www.osho.com
Name: Osho.com.
Description: An outstanding site – articles, multi-media, library, meditation resort, virtual tour, questions, art, insights.

Website : www.damanhur.org
Name: Damanhur.
Description: Visit the extraordinary underground Temple of Mankind, university, news, information, events, courses.

Website : www.jeanhouston.org
Name: The Foundation for Mind Research.
Description: Books, articles, transcripts, details of annual journeys, description of contemporary Mystery school.

Website : thehouseoflife.co.uk
Name: The House of Life
Description: Naomi Ozaniec's website: books, articles, invitation to join a contemporary Mystery School, The House of Life.

Website: www.williambloom.com
Name: William Bloom
Description: Holistic health and spiritual well-being, details of courses and books from one of the UK's leading exponents of the holistic life.

Disclaimer
The publisher has used its best endeavours to ensure that the URLs for external websites referred to in this book are correct and active at the time of going to press. However, the publisher has no responsibility for the websites and can make no guarantee that a site will remain live or that the content is or will remain appropriate.